WHO'S
IN CHARGE OF
"YOUR"
CHURCH?

John J. Clark

KIDZMATTER
PUBLISHING

Who's In Charge Of Your Church?

Published by KidzMatter
432 East Val Lane, Marion, IN 46952

kidzmatter.com

Printed in the United States of America

Cover Design by Andrew Brooks,
andrewbrooks.crtv@gmail.com

Book Layout by Nicole Jones, kneecoalgrace@gmail.com

Edited by Kay Williams

ISBN: 978-1-968198-00-8
ISBN (ebook): 978-1-968198-01-5

Dedicated to the people and leaders of
the Converse Church of Christ.

Table Of Contents

FOREWORD

Scripture asserts that truth is established by the testimony of two witnesses. Over the years, I have proudly stood by while people offered their gratitude for God's powerful goodness at work in the life and words of my dad. I join my testimony to theirs! I affirm the selfless humility that lets God's grace shine through, grace that has grounded our family and has inspired and equipped hundreds of his parishioners. This book distills decades of that hard-won wisdom into a church management plan that is both accessible and transformational. My dad's own ever-increasing dependence on the Holy Spirit for sustenance and direction underscores every lucid explanation and every organizational flow chart in this essential resource. Here, you will find more than an operational handbook for church; you will find a plan for leadership patterned after the very love of Christ -- love that lifts people out of the margins and into their functional purpose as image-bearers of a living God. The principles outlined on these pages offer clear direction for cultivating meaningful corporate worship, efficient administration, and compassionate, effective collaboration, moving us closer to the deep unity that Jesus prayed for in

Gethsemane. I can testify to truth within them and the heart behind them, and I am profoundly grateful that God afforded me a front row seat to the authenticity of their author and the eternal impact of his example.

Dr. Amy (Clark) Linnemann
Executive Director of Beloved
and ever-grateful daughter of the author

"Who's in Charge of Your Church" answers the question we've all been too afraid to ask: Is leading a church REALLY just like leading a business, or is there something more? I've read the books and heard the messages. And, in truth, many times the leadership methodology in our churches is NO DIFFERENT from the secular business world - save for some church jargon and "spiritual" phrases in our mission and vision statements. In this deeply refreshing book, John Clark dares to say the quiet part out loud. If we're HIS Church, then HE needs to be in charge.

For the past 4 years, not only have I come to believe the principles found in this book, but I've also put them into practice. The results have been nothing short of transformative. After nearly 25 years in full-time ministry, this season has been the richest, most satisfying, and most spiritually fulfilling of my ministry life. Our church staff love each other. Our leaders understand Who's in charge. Our congregation is growing in all the ways that matter. I see no reason to ever go back. If you're ready for transformative change in your church or organization, I can give no stronger endorsement for the words that follow.

Joe Wisley
Lead Minister
Converse Church of Christ

PROLOGUE

This book is about management. It is not about theologies, traditions, or methods for successful local ministries. Management is about control, effectiveness, results, and improvement. W. Edwards Deming posited that 85% of workplace problems were management problems. While I agree with Deming regarding business management, I submit, as it relates to the church, that percentage could easily expand to 90% or 95%. There appears to be a great need for the church to come up with a system of management that acknowledges the Holy Spirit as the operational and functional Head of the church.

This book will propose, outline, and explain an uncomplicated management system for any local congregation to be able to recognize The Holy Spirit as the Chief Officer of the church. What I will describe is unlike any system of management about which I am aware in the current contemporary church. What follows represents a lifetime of thinking. My hope is that it will challenge every church to examine its management system and whether adopted in whole or in part, this book will provide the church with a much more effective way to manage itself under the day-by-day operational control of the Holy Spirit.

The Problems

1. *Management structures superimposed on the church from historical tradition and American culture*

The most enduring management structure adopted by the church has been a hierarchy of religious rule-makers and priests positioning themselves between God and mankind. We can find one of the oldest examples in the Catholic church whose multi-layer management structure includes a pope, cardinals, archbishops, bishops, diocese priests, local priests, superior nuns, and nuns. After hundreds of years of existence, Reformers attempted to modify it; however, similar structures were put in place that have also endured for hundreds more years.

In many ways, these reformations simply became imitations of the management structures they were attempting to reform, with hierarchical groups making the rules, creating policies, interpreting theologies, and continuing to position themselves between parishioners and God. As management structures, these have all been successful in one specific way. They have maintained control of the church's thinking, theologies, decision- making, and therefore, the accomplishment of its mission. Out of simple endurance, these structures may be called "successes," but in effectiveness, (other than maintaining strict control), they have been less than successful at true disciple-making.

Other management structures have found their way into the church cultures of America. Because America is governed by a representative form, the church has adopted similar models for its local system of management. Elders, Deacons, Deaconesses, and Ordained Ministers have been voted into positions of authority for local bodies of believers, resulting in layers of management and committee structures that control the church on a local basis. There seems to be a comfort in congregations knowing that they have elected their "best people" to be their decision-makers regarding the mission, vision, and direction for their efforts. (There is probably more scriptural evidence for casting lots than for voting, as it regards finding acceptable leaders for the church.)

It appears that even in what we might term our most successful congregations, (those that have huge numbers of members and massive budgets) we have yet to shake free from management systems that encumber the church and disregard The Holy Spirit as its operational and functional chief officer.

2. *The church's response to the world's consumer/commodity mentality*

The marketplace of the American culture surrounding the church has come to expect decreasing costs, ever improving quality, as well as the meeting of personal needs, expectations, and feelings for every commodity in the marketplace. Around the early 1980's, when the quality revolution hit America, businesses were forced to compete based on consumer requirements, and suppliers were forced to continuously tighten the parameters on acceptable products. The American public reacted with ever increasing expectations. This may have been an unintended consequence, but every business in America felt its effects.

The church has developed a similar mentality and competitive position in its marketplace, and management structures within the church have been forced to accommodate. Churches perceived as successful because of their enormous size have formed teams of executive decision-makers and marketing teams that set targets for their growth (i.e., alpha males between the ages of 25 and 40.)

These highly driven groups of leaders push congregations to attend, give, and invite people into their sanctuaries who are then deemed marketing successes. The resulting growth necessitates management structures similar to their counterparts in business, (i.e., CEO, CFO, CMO, or COO) who supervise the groups of skilled staff who produce results in keeping with the goals of these leaders, or they are dutifully dismissed and replaced. In America, before the advent of Total Quality Management (TQM), we used to call this form Management by Objective (MBO).

Once again, The Holy Spirit's role as the functional Head of the Church is usurped by the presumed needs of the Organization relegating Him to the status of Figurehead, rather than the true operational leader He is designed to be. He may appear at the top of the Organizational chart, but the Executive Team that appears immediately beneath Him really controls the Organization.

(I do not believe there is anything either unbiblical or inherently wrong with megachurches. In fact, many positive kingdom results have come from their powerful ministries. I am only stating that in nearly all of them, management structures have been forced on them either for the expediency of decision-making or continuing market success, which are principles vastly different from those found in the New Testament. These have occurred in response to the consumer mentality which exists in the culture surrounding them and into which their ministries extend.)

3. *Churches ruled by traditions and outdated methods*

If you were able to count them, how many churches in America do you think you could find that are hamstrung with one of the following axioms?

- We've never done it that way.
- We've always done it this way.
- Our best years of success happened when we did it this way.
- We had a problem with one of our leaders, so we now do it this way, so we'll never have a problem like that again.
- A particular family (or committee) has been in charge of that for years; so, we just let them handle it the way they've always handled it.

Because there exists no official standard for management in most churches, many are positioned to maintain the status quo by their histories. Traditions become as important to local members as biblical precedents, some even more important. Because of these traditions, decision-makers attempting to follow the leading of the Holy Spirit are restricted from making the changes many of these churches desperately need to make, some for mere survival.

Traditions come in many forms. Some include perpetuating programming that has long since lost its effectiveness. Others include worship parameters where numbers of prayers, styles of music, numbers of hymns (even the numbers of verses), orders of service, use of or exclusion of certain instruments, and staging requirements (down to the "sacred" positions for communion tables or pulpits). None of these have scriptural precedents, but any of them can stand in the way of change even if change would be suggested by the Spirit. Most represent significant obstacles to the desires of the Holy Spirit for true functionality in the church.

4. *The differences in managerial thinking between lay leaders and vocational ministers*

Most lay leaders in churches understand the role of management in their workplaces and lives. Their vocations may cast them in management roles, or they may be supervised by someone who represents management to them. Either way, they get it.

Lay leaders also understand the terminology used by management when referring to their work. They understand concepts like continuous improvement, meeting quotas, following standards, participation in quality circles, respect for and submission to a boss, working collaboratively with co-workers, working safely, and helping a company achieve its mission and goals. Some would understand terms completely foreign to most ministry-trained people, such as Six Sigma, Kaizen, Kanban, ISO 9000, The Deming Prize, or Malcomb Baldrige Awards.

When lay leaders come to church, they feel very lost when they hear their Ministry Leaders talk in religious language. They hear about flocks, bodies, or kingdoms and the familiarity they feel at work and home goes out the window. They quickly begin to ask questions like, "Who's in charge? Who makes the decisions? How does work get accomplished? How can I fit into this structure so foreign to me?" Frankly, our ministry jargon hasn't gone a long way toward satisfying them.

Equally as frustrated are ministers who have gone through years of ministry training in fine private colleges, which focus on their preparation for ministry, but have given them virtually no tools or training in managing an Organization. These ministers know much about the biblical descriptions of the church from scripture but have no way to put the management ideas they have in their minds into terms or concepts their parishioners understand from their personal perspectives or life experiences.

A stand-off results. Minsters look blankly at their parishioners wondering how to explain what has been taught to them in terms they will understand. Lay leaders push for management systems that resemble the systems in their workplaces, which allow them to be successful and provide methods to measure their success. Issues of workflow, decision-making, reporting relationships, organizational charts, and project management systems lay unresolved, when these are the specific things lay leaders seek. Ministers then complain that their lay leaders are trying to run the church like a business when it is organic and no business model adequately either describes or works for it.

As both sides stare at each other, either someone surrenders or one of these results occur.

- Few people understand what is really going on in the church, much less how to get involved in it.
- The church becomes a business where targets are set, strategic plans are made and followed, and success is measured (generally in budgetary and attendance terms).
- Everyone smiles sweetly, says hello to a group of people with whom they socialize on Sundays, and quits asking the hard questions.
- A stalemate occurs and is allowed to persist, becoming a source of continuous strife.

5. *The need for a management model that lasts longer than a church's last charismatic leader's ideas*

Many churches look longingly at their neighbor's church thinking, "If we could have just hired THAT guy." They see the successes that a particularly gifted, gregarious preacher makes in the life of "his" church and think to themselves that they have the wrong guy in the leadership role of "their" church. In many cases, they're not wrong to think such thoughts.

In many successful contemporary churches, you'll find a pastor who has taken charge and implemented his own version of management, one that he understands and with which he can be effective. His system becomes adopted as the best way to run things. If he is kept in a position to set the agenda, make the most important decisions, and answer all the hard questions about what God wants from the church, things may go rather well. In these cases, it really doesn't matter whether his management system makes sense or is sustainable past his presence, because as long as he remains in the control role, he makes it work.

The resulting problem is obvious and has two distinct outcomes.

- What do you do when he's gone?

    He is the only one who really understands how things are getting done. He is the only one who knows what to measure to ensure continuing success. He is the only one who has the charisma to keep the church motivated toward the goals he sets.

- When he's gone, if you can find an effective replacement, many things will be managed differently during this new leader's tenure because he will now run everything based on his own ideas and charisma.

The church is forced through a process of reorganization in order to give this new leader the space he needs to produce similar results to his predecessor, but with his own management methods. In either case, the church is forced into management upheaval every time a new leader departs or arrives.

6. *The root of division in every church is based on control issues, even if the divisions are couched in biblical or spiritual terms.*

I can think of few, if any, church splits that have occurred where something other than "who gets to be in charge" is the core issue. It doesn't matter if the discussions center on the color of the carpet or whether the Holy Spirit can actually hear the prayers of the unregenerate, look long and hard enough and you'll see past the talk or anger and find people competing for control.

A church occupies one of the greatest positions of power compared to any other organization of which a person may be a part. Eternal destiny is put on the line by the church. The church is where help for marriages and kids is found and where a person's purpose on planet earth is explained. As deep psychological and sociological needs are defined by the church, guilt, fear, freedom, forgiveness, and love are also all put into proper perspective by it.

The church is a place where, absent the control of the Holy Spirit, people are going to compete for the role of Leader. This competition arises from human nature and helps define the need for Someone other than a human being to be in control of it.

Jesus spent His last hours praying for unity among believers. No doubt He could see down the long tunnel of history knowing how terribly good we would become at dividing His Body with our control issues, when He always intended that He would keep it unified by controlling it Himself.

7. *Fear!*

What would the church look like if its people and leaders put the Holy Spirit in charge of the Organization? To most ministers and lay leaders, doing so would represent one of the scariest ideas in the world. When seriously entertaining this idea, their instantaneous question would become, "Who will interpret what the Holy Spirit is saying to the church?" Do you recognize a control issue arising?

Church leaders have been told so many different things about the nature of the Holy Spirit, such as how the Holy Spirit communicates His will and what the true evidences of the Holy Spirit are in the life of a believer or church body, that allowing the Holy Spirit to manage the church scares them to death. Rather than making any real attempt to do so, they substitute something that gives them the feeling of firm footing on which to stand to manage an organism crying out for its Head to be given control.

INTRODUCTION

1. The Format

This is a management handbook, and given the problems outlined so far, as well as the solution proposed, you may now realize what this book is and is not about. It is about management. It is not about what your church believes or does not believe. It is not theological, but it is biblical; however, it should not push you out of your church's comfort zone or teachings about Jesus or salvation. It is also a handbook, which means it is meant to be used and not just read.

It is meant to be pulled off the shelf as a reference tool from time to time. The chapters are numbered and the points in each chapter are delineated, as well. This is done for the purpose of making things easy to find after a read through is complete. You will find the concepts written in this book lean on scriptural precedent and that the priorities of management and the execution of the principles which you uncover closely following the teachings of Jesus, as well as the other New

Testament writers. It will be faithful to the New Testament, but I will not quote many scriptures. There will be a few references made to certain passages of scripture, but you will need to look them up for yourself. What follows is intended to challenge what you may believe you have settled in your heart and mind. It has certainly challenged everything I've seen about management in the church. I won't be telling personal stories or giving you wonderful illustrative materials along the way. I'm simply laying out a management system, compatible with what I read about the New Testament church. That's it.

2. The Language
(Lay Leader Terms, not Ministry Terms)

I will be using lay language more than ministry jargon to explain the principles in this book. The reason for doing so is simple. The numbers of people in every church who understand workplace management terms far outnumbers the people who understand ministry terms. Here is a quick summary of two terms you will find going forward, The Boss and the Organization

3. The Boss

In my way of thinking, God, Jesus, and the Holy Spirit share a brain when it comes to church management theory. Most people know a good boss from a bad one in their workplace, so in this book, I will call the Head of the church, "The Boss." In that light, you should imagine Him to be the best Boss ever! Make no mistake, in management terms, God, Jesus, and the Holy Spirit are The Boss! I hope those of you in the ministry are not offended by this terminology. I guarantee your parishioners know exactly what a Boss is.

4. The Organization

In this book, the term "Organization" will always refer to the church. In management terms it refers to everyone who is, or at least should be, functionally involved in accomplishing the mission of the Organization. I could have used either of the terms company or business, but the word organization has the same root as organism, which is very apt for the church. Most people recognize that if you do not contribute to the Organization for which you work, you don't last long. Church members should respect the Organization called the church, similarly. This Organization has no non-functional parts.

If I use other lay terms for functional parts of the church which you might normally find in books like this, I will explain them as I go. These two (Boss and Organization) are critical to understand from the outset.

5. The Two Sections of the Book

Part One: The Structure
Part Two: The Functionality

Putting all this material together in one place has been quite a challenge. It has existed in various places at different times, but this is the first time it's been pulled together in a book. The presentation of what follows must be unpacked in layers; therefore, I've divided the book into two sections. As the information is rolled out for you, I will attempt to reference the other parts of the book where more details can be found about certain elements. For example, while describing the Structure of the Organization, I will mention the Six Love Languages of the church.

Simply stating them will not explain them for you, so when I mention them, I will reference the later chapter in the book where they are explained in greater detail. In this way, I hope to maintain focus on the points I am making throughout the book and not overwhelm you with details in one section that should be held for later description and discussion.

The first section of the book will describe the overall structure that allows the Organization to see how working relationships function as a whole. Each layer of the Organizational chart (Org Chart) will be described and explained until it's clear how each layer relates to all the others.

The second section will dig deeper into the functionality of the Organization. Corporate folks would understand this as all that goes on between the boxes on the Org Chart. It's in the functionality where many churches get bogged down or confused, so I will take as great care as possible to be clear in these descriptions.

My Personal Journey Into Management

My life experiences have taught me several lessons.

- Respect for authority

    I grew up in a rural subdivision on a street where seventeen boys and one girl lived nearby (poor girl). When disagreements broke out during pickup football games in our yard, my father, an incredibly quiet and principled man, would simply walk into the middle of the game, pick up the football, and carry it into our house without speaking.

    My father was also the vice president and general manager of a factory that made winter coats. One of my favorite activities was to follow him out of his office onto the factory floor when something was on his mind. When he concentrated, his face fell into a very natural frown and the employees didn't understand that face like I did. I enjoyed watching them all scramble to find ways to be busy at something, anything, as he passed them on his way through their workspaces.

- It's the job of the laborers to keep the boss in a position to never have to wait for whatever he needs next.

While in high school and college I worked summers on a custom residential construction crew. It was a small organization with only three or four employees. The boss was also quiet, principled man and a good friend of my father. I recall my first day mixing mortar for the boss, who was also a skilled mason. I arrived on the job at 8:00 and so did he. He stepped up to a very dry mortar board with his trowel in hand and turned and looked at me and quietly said, "This is what we call a dollar waiting on a dime." After scrambling to get mortar on the mortar board and bricks on the scaffolding, I quickly learned my second lesson about authority. (I also arrived at 7:00 the next morning!)

- There is a better method of managing people in ministry than to drive them like a cowhand drives a herd of cattle.

  Soon after graduating from college with a bachelor's in Church Music, I landed my first job as an associate staff member in a church of about nine hundred as the Minister of Music. My boss was the senior minister who was highly skilled at the theory of management known as Management by Objective, which is another way of saying, he set the goals and I did whatever I could to meet them and it seemed I was never really able to satisfy him. That ministry lasted one year.

- Getting everyone to buy into the vision and mission of the Organization is critical to its success.

  My first stint in ministry lasted about thirteen years. Like many music ministers right out of college, I bounced here and there, never lasting long in one place. During these years, I taught music for a couple of different Bible colleges, mainly because I was skilled at training travelling groups to represent the colleges in churches, retreats, and weeks of camp.

During this time, I drove several groups of students to achieve excellence, much like I had been driven by my bosses in the local ministries I had served. I couched my goals in such high-sounding kingdom terms that the impressionable students willingly sacrificed themselves to meet them. I am not proud of myself for that, but the groups were excellent!

- There must be a method of managing things that makes the church function more like the church in the New Testament.

During these years, I also earned a Master's Degree in Ministries and spent four of the thirteen years as the senior minister of a church of about two hundred. I learned several valuable lessons during those four years, not the least of which was a rather harsh one. Every person in a local church feels they have some right to be the boss. This lesson was not a fun one to learn, but unfortunately true. There were successes during that ministry as I began to formulate my own theories on church management. Infantile as they were, they worked in small ways.

For the next 25 years of my career, I left vocational ministry and worked in business; the first 10 years for a manufacturing company; the last fifteen for a service industry firm. My role in the manufacturing company grew from manual labor, through customer service, into quality and training, ending with international distributor relations. During these years, I went back to college and earned an MBA. My personal education in management theory grew exponentially. I underwent 96 hours of Management Representative training for the manufacturing company to become ISO 9000 certified. That business was led and driven by an entrepreneur who, in management terms, made every day an adventure. While with this company, I learned an equal balance of positive and negative lessons about management, all were of great value to me.

For the next 15 years I worked for an architectural/engineering firm who specialized in K-12 school design. Originally, I was hired as a corporate trainer, but quickly moved into the quality side of the business. In that role, I was able to define the baseline process of school design and create measurable points of progress enabling project managers to both predict and track design progress in real time.

Soon after, I was promoted to Chief Human Performance Officer in charge of quality and training. While I worked in these two businesses, I continued to preach and teach in two churches, eight years as a volunteer in one church and seventeen years as a part-time staff member for the other. The management lessons I learned during these years were the most profound of my life.

Negative Lessons:

- Helping a boss achieve his personal goals for the company is the best way to enhance your own career.
- Allowing a Chief Financial Officer to have too much authority in a company may lead to bigger profits, but not always greater missional success.
- On occasion, if certain conditions warrant, company leaders will sacrifice their principles to protect people.

Positive Lessons:

- Respecting and exceeding client expectations leads to long-term success.
- Skills improved by employees in the white spaces between the boxes on the organizational chart are the most critical to their success. This might include such skills as public speaking, conflict resolution, time management, meeting management, or expectations management, as well as others.
- Employees will drive themselves harder because of recognition and attention from the boss than they will from the pay they receive for delivering on work orders or meeting project manager demands.

While learning these and other lessons from my business experience, I was also learning lessons from the two churches in which I taught and preached. I saw both churches labor, somewhat unsuccessfully, with management structures that failed to discover their critical paths to success. I watched groups of elders struggle to come to terms with the realities of what was and was not happening in these two churches.

I observed the principles, processes, and planning that never became clear to the average members of one of these two churches, and its rapidly resulting decline. All the while, I kept learning.

For the last twelve years, I have been working as the senior minister of a church of approximately five hundred located in the Midwest in a small town of 1200. It is here that I have implemented many of the principles found in this book. The elders and leaders have been open to the ideas I have brought with me. Management functionality has been a struggle for them at times in the long history of this congregation, and I am convinced it was God's intention for our paths to cross for such a time as this. My future is bound up in their success. I am learning many things as I grow with them. They are extraordinarily good at loving God and each other.

READ THIS FIRST!

Before we begin, we must agree on three assumptions. If we cannot agree on these assumptions, the foundation comes out from under what follows. All too often I have read the first two or three chapters of a book only to discover that I fundamentally disagree with the underlying assumptions of the author, at which point I usually put the book aside and never finish it. Some books are worth reading anyway! If you have made it this far in this book, there's hope for us!

Assumption One:

Let's agree that although philosophers across history have tried to describe the purpose of humanity in many ways, we'll let the sweep of scripture settle this issue for us. I know other writers of religious books may have used other terms for this, see if we can agree with these:

Humankind's purpose on earth is to Love God Back!

Assumption Two:

This assumption gives us ground on which to stand together about the purpose of the church. American corporations spend inordinate amounts of money and time on retreats where hired consultants simply state the obvious! Your church may have done something like that. Your church also may state this assumption differently or more eloquently, but I'm seeking a basis for agreement here.

The purpose of the church is to help people love God back!

Assumption Three:

I assume you long for your church to function as similarly as possible to the church you find in the pages of your New Testament. I believe you'd like to implement, in some form of management style or structure, the attributes of leadership described by Jesus, so we can agree on this third assumption. You will know that your Organization is healthy when you can read the descriptions of the church in Acts 2:42-47 and Acts 4:32-35 and can say to yourself, "That sounds like my church!" I have distilled the functionality of these verses into six words that will occur throughout this book.

- Adoration
- Transformation
- Companionship
- Compassion
- Partnership
- Evangelism

There are cultural elements of these verses that we cannot duplicate in the contemporary church; but the spirit of these verses certainly can and should be replicated. It is the organizational enthusiasm for the changes Jesus makes in the lives of His followers that we will use as our standard of excellence. We will be building a first-century model of church management, fit for the 21st century.

Book Summary

To summarize all that follows is to keep in mind three factors. Since the church is comprised of people that God holds most dear, they are its greatest strength and, at times, its greatest weakness. In management terms, when people are placed in charge of people, consistency, priorities, and clarity can be manipulated and mishandled. To avoid this, watch for these three factors in the management model that follows.

- Principles
- Processes
- Plans

To effectively manage the church, reliance must be placed on factors that do not bend to the inclinations or whims of people. What is required is the security of factors that do not change. You will notice that I have chosen principles which lock in the character of the church; processes that allow for consistency and measurability of the health of the church; and planning that provides a blueprint for forward progress and effectiveness of ministry. I will return to these three factors in the last chapter of the book as I outline an implementation plan for the content of all that you absorb along the way.

PART 1:
THE STRUCTURE

It is an impossible task to describe the functionality of the church, a very organic group, with an Org Chart.

Are you as amazed as I am, when looking back at the impossible task of leading the children of Israel out of Egypt, that Moses had no more organizational structure than for each person to stick with their kin, clan, and family? There were no camel care groups, no centralization of blanket weaving, no currier group members to relay instructions, and no aid station workers for the chronically fatigued. How on earth did he get this completely disorganized group out of the country? Impossible task? Yes, but he did it!

The church looks like that to me on occasion. God gets things done with way less organization and management than I would have thought necessary; therefore, understand this concept. We will be using extra-biblical mechanisms, like an Org Chart, to describe a very organic functional structure. What we use to describe the structure of the church may fail, but the church will not!

We need to be able to describe the church as an Organization with structure and sensible functionality.

Our western culture demands structure when more than two people get involved in any project. Think about it. Two people decide to take a road trip, and the organizational questions begin. Who decides where we are going? How will we figure out the best way to get there? Where will we stay if it takes more than one day to get there and back? Where and when will we eat? It boils down to who will take charge, and if we can agree on that, then who gets delegated to plan and execute all the logistics? Americans expect structure. Okay, let's get started!

CHAPTER 1
The Org Chart

Everything that follows in this book is based on the structure of this Functional Organizational Chart. It would be best to study it carefully before proceeding.

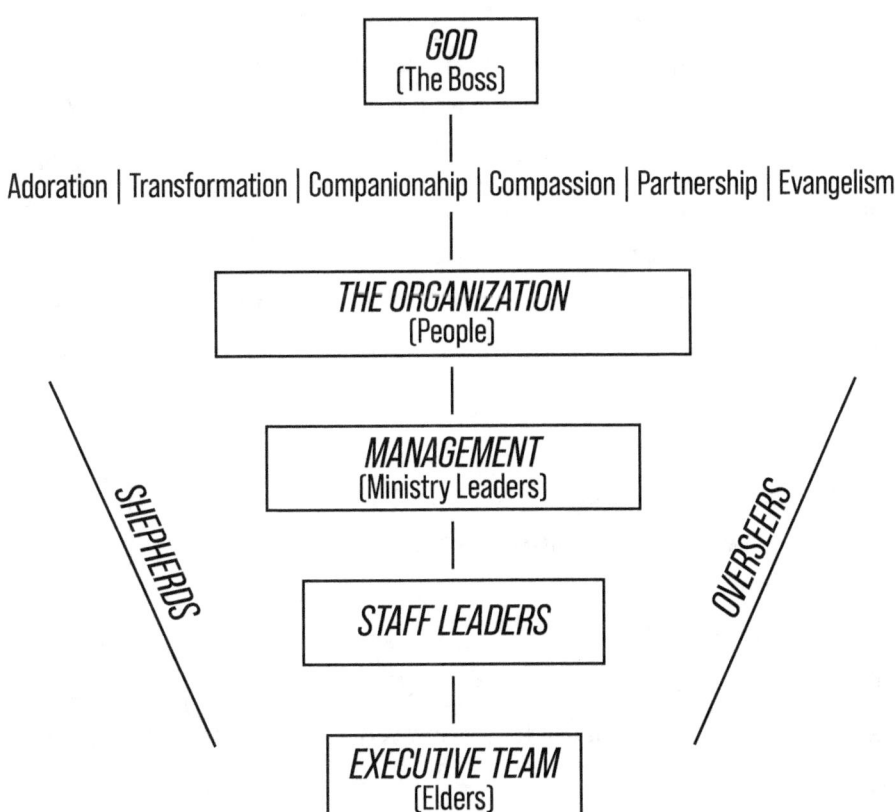

The desire of corporations to invert their organizational charts; and their inability to make it work in the real world.

Business leaders for many years now have seen the need for servant leadership in their companies. If you follow leadership links on the LinkedIn app, you'll routinely see leaders described in such terms. It seems that successful corporations have discovered the model Jesus had in mind for leaders in His kingdom.

Almost no corporations have been able to successfully implement an inverted Org Chart in real time. The problem lies at the top. Without clear direction, without a specific plan, and without one who knows what that plan should be, the chart fails as a management tool. As much as the leadership team of any given company may wish for their managers, executive directors, and vice presidents to see themselves as a support group for their employees, they cannot without someone to communicate clarified targets and goals to the corporation. It's simply not possible for the line level employees to meet, coordinate and focus quickly enough for any given company to stay viable.

The need for church members to know who is in charge, setting the priorities for the Organization

The need in the church is the same. The members of the Organization need someone to direct them toward clearly stated goals. They need to know who will be keeping them focused.

The same companies that would invert their organizational charts, if they could, would also tell you that it is more important to impress upon their employees the guiding principles that are driving the company toward the fulfillment of its mission than it is to dictate work orders to them. The energy and buy-in the leadership team needs from their workers will be volunteered if the employees feel that they are contributing to something bigger than a time clock leading to a paycheck. In a volunteer Organization like the church, it is even more critical that the members give their buy-in to the vision of the Organization. Fortunately, in the church, everyone has immediate and constant access to The Boss!

The reason an inverted Org Chart works for the church:

1. The person laying down the guiding principles, setting the goals, providing the vision is at the top of the chart. It is clear to everyone who is in charge. Quite possibly those who have been identified as leaders in our local congregations have not made clear to our Organizations the exact role The Boss expects to play in the life of the church. His priorities aren't clear to them. We may have made them less clear through our interpretations of them. In some cases, we have substituted other priorities in place of His.

2. An inverted chart allows those deemed leaders by the Organization to see themselves in their roles as servants of the Organization rather than drivers of it. Most local leaders long to respond to the concept Jesus taught when He told his disciples that the greatest among them would be the servant of all. Of Himself, Jesus said that not even

He came to the world to be served, but rather to serve it and give His life as a ransom for it. Most leadership teams in the church wish they could figure out a way to position themselves under the Organization rather than over it. In fact, those who long for positions of control at the top of the chart probably disqualify themselves from being there.

3. It is vital to see this chart in functional terms, not in terms of titles and offices. It is a man-made chart designed to describe the functional layers in the organic church. You will quickly discover that efforts to climb the corporate ladder as you might see on a traditional chart will quickly lead you to lower and lower levels on this one. Each box on the chart describes a function. You will also discover that church leaders have functions in more than one box at a time. They are not relegated to one space or layer on the chart.

The Org Chart Layers

- **The Boss** (God, Jesus, Holy Spirit)
- **The Organization** (the people)
- **Management** (Ministry Leaders, paid and unpaid)
- **The Staff Leader(s)**
- **The Executive Team** (typically elders)

The Boss
God, Jesus, The Holy Spirit

The Boss drives everything. That is such good news for leaders who think they need to drive the Organization forward and have long since grown tired of it. The truth is that everyone in the Organization will respect The Boss and work harder for Him than they will for any church leader. The other good news is that The Boss is directly connected to every individual in the Organization by His presence in their hearts. He is in the perfect position to give specific direction to every member of the Organization 24 hours a day. Furthermore, the Organization must quickly learn that the expectations of The Boss are unrelenting.

The Organization
The People

Many church leaders have difficulty accepting "The People" at the top of the management Org Chart because their experience has taught them that nothing gets done unless they make it happen. That's understandable. Many congregations would be fearful of giving the People the top level of control of the Organization. How will decisions get made? What happens when they come up with hundreds of different ideas and ways to get things done? It will be chaos! Not necessarily. Certainly not if The Boss gets His way. Most people want to please their boss. In the church, they simply haven't been told exactly how to do that.

Management
Ministry Leaders - Paid and Unpaid

In the next section of the book, I will identify the Six Love Languages of the church. For now, just trust that equipping the people to speak love to The Boss is the work of the team of Ministry Leaders of the church. They support the efforts of the people above them to please The Boss. Their watch words are support, serve, help, equip, assist, and encourage.

Staff Leaders

Staff Leader is a role or a function, not an office. Different leaders will routinely occupy the function of this layer of the Org Chart. It represents a role as an equipper of equippers. The people in this box support the efforts of management who are trying to keep those above them focused on speaking the Six Love Languages to The Boss. Staff Leaders minister to Ministry Leaders. They function by the same set of watch words as the layer above them.

The Executive Team
Typically, the Elders; but not always

This layer is the base on which the entire structure above them rests. They support the success of everything going on above them. It is important for those functioning at this level to realize that they are not controlling the efforts going on above them. They are supporting them. Their watch words are shepherding and overseeing. (A better term might be under-seeing.) People functioning here directly support the work of the Staff Leaders, but they keep their eyes on the whole Organization above them.

The Six Love Languages of the Church

These Six Love Languages summarize the Bible's description of the words and actions our Boss's Organization can produce that will result in a church described by the final verses of Acts chapters 2 and 4. These are the guiding principles for His Organization. He waits longingly to hear us speak them to Him. They give us tangible ways to express our love back to Him.

Adoration
Another word for adoration is praise, which is an outward expression of the inward acknowledgement of God as absolutely Sovereign. Biblical worship is never passive; always active. To speak the language of adoration to The Boss means

making it a demonstration, not merely a thought. The people must come to expect from themselves praise as a lifestyle for their Boss, and to recognize it as one of their Love Languages.

Transformation

Transformation means becoming like Jesus. When a disciple followed a Teacher or Rabbi, they spent every minute they could at His feet, learning how He spoke, ate, acted, laughed, cried, walked, interacted, focused, thought, and treated people. They literally spent every waking moment with Him to learn His lifestyle, not just His thoughts and teachings. The Love Language of Transformation is spoken by the people as they allow the Holy Spirit to change their inner person, their character, into the likeness of Jesus.

Companionship

This language is the active demonstration of the "One Anothers" of the New Testament. Chief among them is Love, but many others exist, such as honor, serve, teach, and admonish, live in harmony, be devoted, accept, instruct, agree, greet, bear with, be kind and compassionate, forgiving, submit, encourage, and build up. The people must come to understand that exercising these "One Anothers" speaks love to The Boss. How we treat each other is a Love Language!

Compassion

Compassion means helping hurting people. This Love Language is spoken when the sheep distinguish themselves from the goats or when the Good Samaritan distinguishes himself from the religious guys. People must realize that when they help those who are hurting, they speak love to The Boss.

Partnership

This means partnering with The Boss using the resources He has given us. It's learning about giftedness and putting those gifts to work both inside and outside the Organization. Every person in the Organization uses everything The Boss has invested in them for the betterment of others, to meet needs, and to demonstrate generosity. It includes, but is certainly not limited to, giving or investing money. The people must understand that everything they have is a blessing from The Boss and that partnering with The Boss to accomplish something speaks love to Him.

Evangelism

Evangelism in which the church is engaged is the act of giving the Good News about Jesus to anyone who needs it, and everyone does. This action fulfills the mission of the Organization and speaks volumes of love to The Boss who authored salvation. It does not stop with spreading the Word but follows through into disciple-making.

The further down you go on the chart, the higher the levels of spiritual strength you must find.

One of the unique features of this Org Chart is the inversion of spirituality along with the inversion of functionality. It is critical to understand this organizational structure in terms of spiritual maturity, as well as the functions of the layers. It is inverted so that the strongest and most mature Christians appear at the bottom of the chart rather than the top.

Most church leaders have longed for a position at the bottom of the Org Chart, rather than at the top. Their inner desire is to be able to follow Jesus' example when, during His disciples' argument about who would become the greatest in the kingdom, He took off His outer garment, grabbed up a towel and basin of water, and began washing their feet. Leaders long to take a seat at the back of the room and be invited to the front rather than being uncomfortably forced to the front because they are seen by the Organization as the leaders.

It is interesting to note in the lists of qualifications for elders and deacons, very few have to do with managerial skills while many are directed at their spiritual maturity. No matter how your church may handle its selection process, I doubt very few highly skilled and successful workplace managers are disqualified from leadership due to their lack of spiritual maturity. Ministerial students are often faced with this ethical question in their practical ministries classes. "Is it better for the church to have a few elders who are spiritually deficient rather than have no elders at all?"

To be qualified to descend to the bottom of this inverted Org Chart, spiritual strength is not optional. It is REQUIRED.

One who has not proven in their homes, communities, and within the Organization that they understand and can fulfill the expectations of The Boss should not be given the privileges afforded to those in the bottom layer of the chart.

Each level down on the chart determines its success by the success of the layer above it.

As with any corporation, the lower levels on the Org Chart work to make the upper levels successful. Parishioners who work in the secular world easily understand this concept. A person may or may not like their supervisor, but they know they cannot succeed in their job or their career path without making them successful. So, it is with our inverted Org Chart.

The people must please The Boss who resides at the top of the chart. The functions of their layer are clear, as are the expectations of The Boss. He wants to be loved in the languages He has prescribed in the teachings of the New Testament. The Six Love Languages are a condensed description of those New Testament teachings. It is the responsibility of the people in their top layer to speak love directly to Him. Those serving the Organization as Ministry Leaders in the Management layer cannot see themselves as successful if the people above them are not equipped, trained, and given ample opportunities to speak the Six Love Languages to The Boss. The success of the Management layer is determined by the success of the layer above them.

Likewise, those serving in the Staff Leader layer cannot see themselves as successful unless the Ministry Leaders in the Management Layer above them have everything they need to succeed. Resourcing them, training them, encouraging them, and building them up is their responsibility. Staff Leaders should never deem themselves a success with unsuccessful Ministry Leaders working above them.

The Executive Team at the bottom of the chart must have such copious amounts of love for the Organization functioning above them that they could never sit by while some part of it struggles to succeed. They completely disqualify themselves from functioning at the bottom of the chart if while shepherding and overseeing the Organization above them, they dispassionately watch some part of it fail.

CHAPTER 2
The Boss

Every Descriptive Model of the Church in Scripture Makes God, Jesus, and the Holy Spirit, The Boss!

We in the church have lost sight of the operational control our Boss would like to maintain over His Organization. He has been relegated to a role most people would recognize as Chairman Emeritus. That is someone who at some point in the history of the Organization was a terrific employee who worked him or herself through the CEO role into a position on the Board of Directors. Eventually, he or she became the chairman of that board, retired, and was given an honorary title. Everyone now working in the Organization enjoys seeing this person from time to time, sings his/her praises, and pretty much ignores his/her old stories and ideas. That is the role we seem to give God in the contemporary church so that He really doesn't have much to do with the day-to-day operation of the Organization.

That description flies in the face of the descriptions we find in scripture about God's role in the church. When Paul describes the church as a functioning human body with hands, ears, and eyes, He describes Jesus as the Head. The head of a human body has everything to do with every action taken by it every second, every minute, every day, whether voluntary or involuntary!

When Jesus describes His collective followers as a kingdom, He reserves the role of king for Himself. A king makes the laws, sets the boundaries, and lays down the principles by which the kingdom will function. In a kingdom, no one other than the king thinks that by their own authority, they can incorporate new decision-making structures in that kingdom which do not involve the king. Doing so would mean immediate demotion or expulsion by the king.

When Jesus refers to His followers as sheep who know His voice, He identifies Himself as the Good Shepherd. He says sheep will not follow any other voice but His own. They cower and are fearful of any other voice. When the New Testament writers use familial terms to identify the church, they never place anyone but God in the role of the Father.

We get no indications from the New Testament that God has ever given up His role as the operational and functional Boss of the Organization. It's past time that we, by our words, actions, and structures, acknowledge His role as The Boss, a role He has never abdicated.

God's Desire to Lead His People in Every Covenant Era, Including the Contemporary Church

Throughout history, no matter the covenant era, in terms of the leadership of His people, God has placed Himself in charge and asked one thing from His people. Trust Me!

Adam and Eve: God tells them He has made the Garden of Eden for them and along with it one rule. Don't eat of the tree in the middle of the garden. He positions Himself as the One in charge, making the rules and telling His children. Trust Me.

Noah: God tells Noah that He is going to destroy the earth and all the people in it. He is in charge, and it will be His doing. God gives Noah instructions about saving himself and his family and in so many words is saying to him, "Trust Me!"

Abraham: Abraham is told that he will be the father of a nation that will show the world how to love God back. God tells Abraham that the promise will come through his son, Isaac, but not many years after Isaac is born God asks Abraham to sacrifice Isaac. With this challenge God is saying to Abraham, "Trust Me!"

Moses: When God calls Moses to deliver the children of Israel out of Egypt, Moses gives Him all manner of excuses as to why he is the wrong guy for the job. In the face of his reluctance, God gives Moses all the reasons He should trust Him.

In Egypt, on the edge of the Red Sea, at Mt. Sinai, and in the wilderness, God, by His daily provision required one thing of Moses and His people. Trust Me!

On the day God began the church, He took charge of the circumstance. He invaded it with His Spirit who took compete control. The sermon God wanted preached was preached. The people who responded, He added to the church. In the days and weeks that followed, He protected His disciples from persecutions. He called Paul into service. God revealed the teachings that He thought were the most important for the Organization to the Apostles and others. Everyone involved in the spread of the church was taught the same lesson by their Leader. Trust Me!

Do we think God has lost interest in His people? Do we think His ideas are now outdated? Do we believe that if WE take charge of getting people to attend OUR worship services and WE divide them into controllable sub-groups, God can then have His chance to do His thing? Do we think some-how God has lost His touch and does not understand how to manage a staff of paid and unpaid Ministry Leaders in the contemporary church? Imagine God leaning over the walls of heaven looking longingly into His church and whispering in a still small voice, "Trust Me."

Keeping The Boss in His Role

To borrow from the title of one of my favorite manage-ment books, Steven Covey's, Principle-Centered Leadership, our Boss is the ultimate principle-centered Leader! To follow management links, listen to leadership podcasts, read organi-zational books, or observe successful corporations these days means running into a variety of principles. Great leaders lead with unshakeable, immoveable principles. Our Boss is the best leader ever!

Privately, I once asked the CEO of a firm for which I worked, "What are the pillars of success on which this company rests?" Without hesitating, he rattled off these five pillars.

- Client Satisfaction
- Business Innovation
- Quality Designs
- Profit
- Employee Satisfaction

I was amazed for two reasons. First, that he knew exactly what would make the company a success and could so quickly and succinctly articulate it. Second, that there was no wall, document, strategic plan, or business card which listed any of those five pillars. Those were the guiding principles of success for the company he was leading, and virtually no one working for him knew them.

In my estimate, no boss in any company has given more attention to the principles which will make His Organization successful than our Boss. This fact makes poor attitudes, disorganization, failed working relationships, and ineffectiveness of many churches a complete mystery to me. This same fact might challenge many churches whose successes are well-recognized to look carefully at the measurements of success they are using, as they may be succeeding more as a corporation producing attendees and giving units than at disciple-making.

Make no mistake, our Boss has laid down His pillars of success carefully and completely. His expectation, that we will follow Him and function by His principles has not changed or relented. His pillars of success continue to have the ability to produce the results He seeks. They cannot be challenged by anyone in His Organization. He is The Boss. He is in charge. The demand for His Organization to meet His expectations is not optional. It is required. Period.

Let's re-summarize our Boss's pillars of success. Our Boss expects to hear our love for Him from us. I think people forget that God has His own set of love languages. As Gary Chapman lays out in his book, *The Five Love Languages*, communication sometimes breaks down in relationships because we speak love to each other in languages that are not understood. One person is listening for love to be spoken in words of affirmation, while their spouse is speaking love to them in quality time. It's as if one is speaking Spanish and the other is listening for German.

Let's review the six pillars of the Love Languages our Boss is longing to hear from us.

Adoration

In his book, *The Hallelujah Factor*, Jack Taylor lays out a case for praise in the life of the church like few writers I have read on this subject. His list of Hebrew and Greek words translated either "praise" or "along with praise" in scripture makes one understand God's desire to be worshipped in spirit and truth. Permeating the lists are expressions like shout, shout of joy, dance, skip about, bend the knee, prostrate, bow, sing, exalt, play the instruments, rejoice, and give thanks. Without question, one of the ways God recognizes our love for Him is in our worship expressions. Whether personal, private, or harmoniously in corporate settings, God loves to receive authentic and passionate adoration from His people. When we release our praises to Him, He hears us love Him back!

Transformation

When we allow the Holy Spirit to transform our characters into the likeness of Jesus, God hears us speak love to Him. Some of the phrases used in scripture to describe our relationship with the Holy Spirit, who comes to dwell in each of our hearts when we are born again are "led by," "live by," "heart set on," "minds controlled by," and "in step with" Him. The evidences of the Holy Spirit's influence on us are easy to see. We bear His fruit!

The nine spiritual qualities listed in Galatians 5:22-23, (love, joy, peace, patience, kindness, goodness, faithfulness, gentleness, and self-control) form a basis of transformation that could keep a disciple of Jesus busy for a lifetime. Add to them others from Colossians 3 like humility, compassion, and forgiveness. When we exhibit these characteristics, God sees us becoming more and more like Jesus, and He hears us love Him back.

Transformation must always occur in line with the clear teachings of scripture. It is imperative that the congregation realize that fact and make concerted efforts to read, study, and memorize scripture, so their character development always conforms to it. The Holy Spirit will never say a thing in a person's heart that is different from what He has already said in scripture. He is never divided against Himself.

Companionship

Our Boss cares deeply about how we treat each other. When Jesus was restoring Peter in John 21, the linkage between our love for Jesus and our concern for each other became apparent. Jesus was telling Peter if you want to love me you must show it in the way you treat others. It is amazing how often this love language is either presumed or ignored in the leadership circles of the church. In staff or elder's meetings, we act as if this love language is for the rest of the Organization, but not here and not now. We've got programming to discuss, calendars to justify, finances to audit, and sometimes, turf to protect, all to please a Boss whose expectation is to hear us speak love to Him by the way we treat each other. How tragic is that?

Compassion

Jesus never met a hurting person that did not pull at His heartstrings. He wants His Organization to respond to the world in the same way. The language of compassion will literally be put to the test on the day of judgment. God will call into question our sympathies and empathies for the hurting people in the world around us. When we care for and meet the needs of hurting people, He says we've cared for Him and met His needs. When we lock eyes with people in the world and find ourselves turning away in shame or disgust, we are turning our eyes away from opportunities to speak love to our Boss. This Love Language is obviously extremely important to Him.

Partnership

When the Holy Spirit takes residence in our hearts, He comes bearing gifts! When discussing management in the church, the list that describes functionality best comes from Romans 12. The functional gifts described there are prophesying, serving, teaching, encouraging, giving, leading, and showing mercy. I will discuss how to discover giftedness later in the book. The point here is to realize that being gifted binds us to our Boss in partnership.

When He brings gifts into our lives, He expects a return on His investment. He makes that clear in Matthew 25 when Jesus tells the parable about the servants and their talents. Our Boss hears us speak love to Him when we use what we have been given to partner with Him in His kingdom.

Evangelism

Our Boss is on a quest, a quest that will end when He knows that no one else will respond to His Good News. It is clear in II Peter 3:9. that the return of Jesus is not something God is artificially delaying, but that He is being patient not willing that any should perish, but that everyone should come to repentance. When we join our Boss in His quest, He hears us speak love to Him. Just before Jesus ascended to heaven having accomplished His task on earth, He put evangelism in terms with which we are all familiar. Go! Make disciples! This Love Language speaks to the very heart of the mission of the Organization.

When the Organization is good at speaking these Six Love Languages, it can be regarded as healthy. Speaking them is clear evidence The Boss is in His role and the Organization is responding to His leadership. Measurements for speaking the Love Languages will be addressed in the second section of this book focused on functionality.

Showing respect for The Boss is an expectation in every gathering of any part of the Organization. He is always present. His expectations are unrelenting. It is not only appropriate to speak love to The Boss on every occasion and in every circumstance, it is imperative. There only need to be two people present on any given occasion for The Boss to think a meeting has been called, and He expects to attend every meeting in His Organization. He's never late, always interested, and always attentive. At every meeting, He waits to see if we will speak love to Him as that's how He knows we regard Him as The Boss!

CHAPTER 4
The Role of Management

1. The Servant Leader Model vs. Management by Objective

The Management layer of the Org Chart is for Ministry Leaders. Whether paid or unpaid, the workers in this layer of the Organization exist to make the layer above them successful at speaking love to God. They serve the layer above them. They do not drive it toward artificially established objectives, like attendance goals, numbers of special events produced, or visitor information collected.

These are responsibility-driven people who respond directly to the conviction of The Boss. They are gifted by The Boss to see the needs of the Organization through His eyes. They have honed skills to help the second layer of the Organization more perfectly speak love to God.

In the days of management by objective, supervisors would be given strategic targets to hit in order to feel successful. They would know that maintaining their role in the organization was dependent on their ability to produce quotas, increase sales, or make improvements that increased either the gross revenue or net profit of the company. There are churches that still handle people who function at this level with objective-driven goals. It's a business model that has been replaced and a management model that has no place in the church.

In the church, Ministry Leaders are asked what the Holy Spirit is guiding them toward in the execution of their ministries, not told by a supervisor what the Organization expects from them. They are allowed to love and serve the people in the Organization in the layer above them. Many of them consider this privilege God's calling in their lives. They thrive when they are allowed to let The Boss inspire them. They burn out, give up, or endure unending frustration when they are driven by artificial objectives and people who think it is their job to force them to achieve these goals.

2. Ministry Leaders stay spiritually sharp, and lead by example.

Qualifications for functionality in the management or third layer of the Organization are multifaceted.

- Ministry Leaders are personally good at speaking the Six Love Languages. There may be some that are better at that than others, but each of them can capably speak them all. Because of this, they have mutual affection for one another. They easily collaborate with one another and are expected to do so. They support one another. As Romans 12 states it, they belong to one another.

- Ministry Leaders are examples to the layer above them in conduct and speech. The words of their mouths and the thoughts of their hearts are pleasing to their Boss, and the people with whom they work can see it and because of that they aspire to it. In their relationships with others in layer three, they demonstrate the possibilities the kingdom holds for those who take the leadership of The Boss seriously. The fruit of the Spirit is offered freely to those alongside whom they work.
- Ministry Leaders recognize the giftedness of those in layer two above them. They know when they find a person with a gift of teaching, encouraging, serving, or leading, for example. They respect those gifts as having come from The Boss.
- Ministry Leaders are equippers. They know the importance of training people in the use of their gifts. They refuse to simply stuff people into places in programming and then wait for them to fail. Doing such a thing is abhorrent to them.

Ministry Leaders are special people and every person in the body of Christ retains the possibility of being one of these leaders. The process of discovery will be explained later.

Ministry Leaders lead the Organization into deeper levels of unity by the example they set every day in the course of interaction with other Ministry Leaders in the Organization.

I will be introducing a method for increasing intimacy with God through accountability partnerships. Management level Ministry Leaders in The Boss's Organization are terrific at maintaining intimacy with Him and are good at helping others to develop that intimacy, as well.

3. Responsibility within the Org Chart flows multi-directionally.

Most organizational charts are unidirectional as they regard reporting relationships, decision-making authority, and workflow. Our chart works differently.

A Ministry Leader may be leading an effort to equip members of the Organization in a particular demographic group to speak love to The Boss in one or all of the languages. A worship leader may be very focused on the Language of Adoration with a restricted group of musicians, while a children's minister in the same church is focused on teaching all the children to speak all Six of the Love Languages.

In our Boss's Organization, Ministry Leaders never function in isolation from each other. There is no turf to protect. As long as a Ministry Leader is focused on pleasing The Boss by equipping people in the Body of Christ to speak love to Him, there is no jealousy or lines of authority within or among the people in the management layer. The particular language on which they are focused, group with which they work, or even their seniority in the Organization gives them no over or under leverage regarding those who work around them. This would include paid versus unpaid Ministry Leaders, as well.

As Ministry Leaders do their work, they understand how to stick with their plans and stay within their budgets. They know they have the freedom to make decisions for their ministries within those limits and any time they are going to move outside those limits, they must inform everyone who may be affected. They are collaborative and cooperative people. They play well with others.

4. Ministry Leaders understand how to manage people well!

Everyone working in the Management level of the church is good at working with people. They employ four principles of people management.

- **Ministry Leaders Care.**

    I can't count the numbers of Ministry Leaders in the church who have the bad habit of using the phrase, "I don't care." Whether they use it about people, resources, programming, or the arrangement of chairs in a room, when they use this phrase, they create an immediate disconnect with those around them. People who serve in the management layer of the church must lose this bad habit and never use that phrase.

    Ministry Leaders care! They care more about the people working with them than the work those people produce. When a person perceives that what they produce is of more interest than who they are to the one leading them, two things result.

    » They quickly understand that if they can find another Ministry Leader who will reward them more tangibly for the same work, they'll change ministry efforts.

» They'll stop innovating because they know that no one cares whether they innovate or not.

Both results are bad for the Organization. Therefore, in the church all Ministry Leaders must care! They care for the layers above and below them, and they demonstrate their concern for others in words and actions. Caring for someone does not mean overlooking their failures or enabling their weaknesses. It is not caring to allow someone to repeatedly fail without addressing those failures nor is it helpful to allow a person to wallow in their weaknesses or to always fix their mistakes for them. Ministry Leaders care for people and want what is best for them.

• **Ministry Leaders eliminate the obstacles keeping people from success.**

When a Ministry Leader sees someone struggling to succeed, particularly in layer two of the Org Chart, they do what is necessary to facilitate success by eliminating obstacles keeping them from success. Do they need resources, training, clearer expectations, or better information? The effective Ministry Leader searches until they discover the obstacle and do whatever necessary to remove it.

This does not mean they intervene in a way that removes the responsibility for speaking each of the Six Love Languages from any individual. It means clearing a path for them to do so.

- **Ministry Leaders utilize the gifted while balancing the load.**

    In the church and in business, it's easy to find self-motivated, internally driven people on which to hang generous amounts of the burden. Ministry Leaders must not do that! They must be good at recognizing gifts and providing people with opportunities to use them, while at the same time protecting them from overburdening and burn out. They balance the load, making sure all plates are full with no plate carrying so much that it breaks down the joy of speaking love to God for anyone in layer two.

    Ministry Leaders recognize that every person in the Organization must be given opportunity to speak all Six Love Languages. They exist to give opportunities to everyone to do that. Even if they lead a ministry with a focus on one or more languages, they encourage those with whom they work the joy of speaking all of them.

- **Ministry Leaders provide performance feedback.**

    Ministry Leaders know their planned outcomes and are generous with their praise when people help them achieve those outcomes. They are also willing to address failures. Ministry Leaders speak love to The Boss by complimenting positive contributions and by working to overcome failures in their area of ministry. People management is addressed more fully in the functionality section of this book.

5. Ministry Leaders complete the answers to the seven questions for the Master Plan.

In our description of organizational structure, the functionality of what I am proposing hangs on a Master Plan. This plan is not a plan typical of most strategic plans, which include market studies, economic forecasts, and other trends that affect outcomes. It is simply a compilation of the intentions of every Ministry Leader in a local congregation known as the Master Plan.

By answering seven specific questions, every Ministry Leader in the management layer of the Org Chart exposes their plan to everyone in the Organization. The plan is developed each year for the following year.

Every Ministry Leader develops an annual plan out of their intense desire to see the Organization speak the Six Love Languages to The Boss, under the guidance of the Holy Spirit in an effort to accomplish the best outcomes imaginable in their areas of responsibility.

Functionality of Ministry Leaders:
- They work from lists of areas of responsibility, not job descriptions.
- They develop annual plans to which they are committed. If/when changes are proposed or become necessary mid-year, Staff Leaders get more directly involved in their success.
- From these plans, budgets are developed and methods established.

- The Organization above them on the Org Chart has total access to their plans.
- All Ministry Leaders, whether paid or unpaid, participate in this process.
- If a Ministry Leader is either unwilling or unable to continue a ministry from one year to the next:
  » Another Ministry Leader is sought by talking to The Boss and the Organization, or...
  » The ministry is discontinued, or...
  » The Executive Team determines that the area of responsibility is so critical to the health of the Organization that a new Ministry Leader is found from outside the Organization.

There are seven questions every Ministry Leader answers to form the Master Plan. The name and contact information of the Ministry Leader should be posted in the header.

- How does this ministry contribute to speaking love to The Boss? Does it focus on one language more than the others? If so, which ones? Why? (Adoration, Transformation, Companionship, Compassion, Partnership, Evangelism)
- Is there a specific segment of the Organization on which this ministry focuses? If so, please identify it and explain why. (i.e., senior saints, musicians, children, youth, men, women, couples, singles, building and grounds)
- Briefly outline the functionality of this ministry. What does it accomplish? (i.e., It feeds and clothes needy people. It prepares and leads weekly worship. It's a Bible Study. It aids in the process of divorce recovery.) Provide

sufficient details that a new member of the Organization would get a good idea of how the ministry functions to know whether or not they might volunteer to be a part of it.

- How will success be measured in this ministry? What are the expected outcomes from it? In what ways will it please The Boss?
- What are the building use requirements of this ministry? Did this ministry have a budget last year? What is the proposed budget this year for this ministry?
- Is this a new ministry? If this ministry was included in last year's Master Plan, are there significant changes proposed for this year? Are there new goals, expansion, or contraction?
- Briefly outline the training plan for incorporating new volunteers into this ministry

The compiled answers to these questions form the Master Plan each year for the Organization. If someone in the Organization either aspires to lead an existing ministry or to start a new one, they are required to answer these questions in order for that ministry to become part of the Master Plan.

The Organization works the plan every year guided and directed by principles and plans and under the control of The Boss.

6. Ministry Leaders undergo annual reviews.

No one in the Organization should ever fear a personnel review, especially Ministry Leaders. There is no cause for fear because they are being driven by their allegiance to The Boss and nothing or anyone else. Since they establish their own targets and success measurements, they need not fear talking about them with those who support them. A time of review is a time for personal assessment, not outside evaluation. Ministry Leaders should look forward to talking about their passions for their ministries. If their passions have waned, this process may help to discover the reason and what steps can be taken to regain those passions. All Ministry Leaders should answer these questions at least once every year.

- While submitting to the leading of the Holy Spirit, how well have my efforts helped the church speak the Six Love Languages to The Boss?
- Having established my own success criteria in my areas of responsibility, how well did I hit my targets for the year?
- How is my intimacy with God? Is my personal walk with Him, my connection to Him, and my ability to sense His leadership in my life going well?
- How clearly do I see the vision and goals for my areas of responsibility? Is the leadership of The Boss and my understanding of the expectations I am trying to meet giving me a clear picture of what I am attempting to accomplish?

- Am I still fully engaged with the people with whom I serve? Do we laugh and cry, discuss and make decisions together freely and openly?
- How would I rate my personal passion for ministry in general at this juncture?
- Are there new areas of ministry toward which The Boss is leading me as I view my long-range future with this Organization? If so, what are they?

7. Ministry Leaders allow themselves to be undergirded by Staff Leaders and the Executive Team.

Simply looking at the Org Chart would give some people pause, thinking that Ministry Leaders are on a higher level than Staff Leaders and Executive Team members. They are. In the traditional sense, the lower levels are direct reports to them and have less decision-making authority than the layers above. A uniqueness of this Org Chart is that mutual sub-mission is calculated as a strength, a spiritual strength. The deeper into the chart you go, the more spiritual strength you find. Those at the bottom of the chart are deemed to be the spiritual leaders of the Organization. They are given respect by the Organization not by their authoritative position over it on the chart, but by the willing submission of the layers above them because of their demonstrated spiritual strength.

Therefore, Ministry Leaders willingly allow themselves and their success to be undergirded by the Staff Leaders and Executive Team members below them. They recognize that the prayers and support given to them from below them are for their good and for their success. They are given confidence of this by the temperament and conduct of these leaders. They are consistently assured that people serving in the layers of the Organization under them will not criticize, critique, or demean them. Therefore, the Ministry Leaders are never given reasons to pull rank or exercise their presumed authority over these Staff Leaders who, by definition, are there to make and keep them successful.

From time to time, Ministry Leaders will find themselves approached by Staff Leaders and Executive Team members for the exercise known as John's Accountability Model, which can be found in The Functionality section of this book (Page 185). This partnership will be requested for their benefit, and they should receive the invitation as such, as they are being undergirded by it. Their spiritual intimacy with The Boss is at the heart of the invitation.

Ministry Leaders should be asked routinely if they have everything they need for success by people serving The Boss in the layers below them on the Org Chart. Humble, honest answers to these questions will only help them, never hurt them. In Numbers 12:3, the Bible states that Moses, one of the greatest leaders of all time, was known as the most humble man on the face of the earth.

On occasion, Ministry Leaders may run out of ideas or begin to lose their passion for their area of responsibility. They should feel confident in these times that the layers underneath them will do everything they can to refresh, inspire, pray for, and provide training for them. They should be encouraged to form relationships with and access support from other Ministry Leaders in sister congregations who are doing similar kinds of ministry. No Ministry Leader should ever fear a conversation about his or her success with any Staff Leader or Executive Team member…EVER!

CHAPTER 5
The Staff Leaders

The layers of the Org Chart represent functions, not particular people. They are not intended to give particular people titles under which to do their work. It is important to remember that the same person may function in more than one layer at a time. Everyone in the Organization has a place in the "People" box in the second layer of the chart. Some are called to work in the "Ministry" layer, the third layer of the chart, too. Some of those who find themselves in the third layer will function in the fourth layer, the Staff Leader layer, as well. Organizations often find that the size and scope of their ministries require full-time paid Staff Leaders. Those same Staff Leaders will find others with them in that layer as they lead their ministries.

Many children's ministers spend a vast majority of their time recruiting, training, and leading adult volunteers. Although their ministry is focused on teaching children to speak the Six Love Languages, their work is less with children than it is with adults. In functional terms, they are Staff

Leaders working with Ministry Leaders who are working with a particular demographic group in the Organization to help them speak the Six Love Languages to The Boss. They are, therefore, functioning in the fourth layer of the chart. When they work with their adults, they are Staff Leaders. When they work directly with children, they are Ministry Leaders. When they join with the children to speak one of the Six Love Languages to The Boss, they participate in the functionality of second layer of the Org Chart.

Everything that was written about the functionality of Ministry Leaders in the last chapter applies to Staff Leaders, as well. The qualitative attributes, functionality, character traits, and intimacy with The Boss all apply to Staff Leaders, as well as Ministry Leaders. Staff Leaders manage people with the same four principles as Ministry Leaders.

- They care.
- They eliminate obstacles inhibiting success.
- They manage the load.
- They provide performance feedback

Staff Leaders complete the same forms that are inserted into the Master Plan, answering the same seven questions as Ministry Leaders. They are reviewed annually by the same seven review questions as Ministry Leaders. If they function as a Ministry Leader, as well as a Staff Leader, they will file a second or third form for the Master Plan for those ministries.

Staff Leaders discover their giftedness in the same way the entire Organization discovers theirs. (See Chapter 13, Page 197.) Qualities of character, connection, and responsibility to

The Boss, and the attachment of those qualities to the Holy Spirit are the same for Staff Leaders as for everyone in the Organization. Everything that applies to layers two and three, applies to layer four! There are, however, a few unique qualities of leadership required of Staff Leaders.

- Staff Leaders model for Ministry Leaders and the people of the Organization a level of spiritual maturity to which everyone may aspire. Paul said, "Follow me as I follow Christ." He was saying, I will model for you what you should want to become as a disciple of Jesus. Becoming a disciple of Jesus necessitates eliminating a few negatives.
  - » You won't find Staff Leaders expressing anger toward Ministry Leaders or other people in the Organization. Staff Leaders know how to manage their anger and not let the sun go down on it.
  - » You won't hear Staff Leaders dredging up old failures of Ministry Leaders or people in the Organization. Staff Leaders know how to deal with failure, make corrections, offer forgiveness, put up with the failings of the weak, and keep moving forward while not looking back.
  - » You won't catch Staff Leaders undermining the ministries of Ministry Leaders by participating in conversations laced with complaints or criticisms which amount to gossip. If they have an issue with a Ministry Leader, they'll talk to that Ministry Leader, not *about* them behind their back.
  - » You won't find Staff Leaders who are weak at speaking one or more of the Love Languages. Staff

Leaders know the languages, practice them, participate in them, and encourage others to do so.

» You won't find Staff Leaders pulling rank on the Ministry Leaders they support. Staff Leaders know their place underneath Ministry Leaders and will not attempt to correct them aside from their departure from the plans and principles that are running the Organization and pleasing The Boss. (See Chapter 7, Page 115)

If Staff Leaders have a concern about a particular Ministry Leader, they will draw close to them instead of stepping back from them. In practical ways, they will encourage them and use John's Accountability Model for improving their intimacy with God. (See Chapter 12, Page 185.) A Staff Leader's instinctive concern is the spiritual well-being of a disengaged or discouraged Ministry Leader. Staff Leaders model how to do justly, love mercy, and walk humbly with God. (Micah 6:8) Staff Leaders know how to get in step with and stay in step with the Holy Spirit and are models of love, joy, peace, patience, kindness, goodness, faithfulness, gentleness, and self-control. (Galatians 5)

• Staff Leaders understand how to lead with influence. Influential leaders are not coercive, do not demand their way, and don't force compliance. Instead, they influence the Organization, leading first by example, then by asking the kinds of questions that direct Ministry Leaders in the Organization back to their responsibilities, plans, and goals. They focus Ministry Leaders on the things they have previously stated are important to them. Staff Leaders always protect the relationship that already exists between Ministry Leaders and The Boss. They let The Boss control and drive the Organization to success. Staff Leaders know that Ministry Leaders will push themselves more in response to The Boss than anyone else, never positioning themselves between the two.

- Even if Staff Leaders are given authority to pass judgment (up to and including hiring and firing), they do not carry out their function by that authority. They serve as designated leaders instead. Understanding that their role on the Org Chart places them under the functionality of Ministry Leaders, they perform their Staff Leader function as one designated to do so from within

the team, not over the top of it. If they are appointed to run staff meetings, their goal is to seek ways to support and assist the team members, not to drive, manage, or control them. They understand that Ministry Leaders will drive for success much more willingly and intensely when driven by The Boss rather than by Staff Leaders.

Managing Performance Failure

When a Staff Leader needs to approach performance failure by a Ministry Leader, they work through a specific plan. Long before any form of discipline is applied, they talk to the person. In fact, a good Staff Leader will not sit down at his or her own desk in the morning without the confidence that every Ministry Leader working in the scope of their watch care has everything they need to be successful within their part of the Master Plan. If a Staff Leader does not have a sense of comfort about a particular Ministry Leader, timely follow-up is critically important. A Staff Leader cannot sit by and watch a Ministry Leader fail.

Long before a Staff Leader is forced to discipline someone, they will be in supportive conversations with them. If there is no trail of conversations about performance in the history of a struggling Ministry Leader, there are no grounds for discipline. To do otherwise would incur an irrecoverable loss of credibility in the life and role of the Staff Leader. It is important to note that every Ministry Leader in the Organization is handled with exactly the same process when it comes to performance failure. No one is an exception, and no one is exempt. The Staff Leader manages the disciplinary process precisely the same way for everyone…no matter what.

If after repeated conversations, a Ministry Leader needs a performance failure formally addressed, the first step is that the Staff Leader accepts full responsibility for that failure. If you are a Staff Leader, you probably (under your breath, of course), just said, "WHAT?! WHAT DID HE JUST SAY?!" Yes, the Staff Leader accepts full responsibility. If the Staff Leader's role is to assure success in the layer just above them, then they must be willing to accept responsibility for the failures in that layer, as well. Be assured that the process of discipline does not stop there. The details and rationale will be explained in the functionality section of his book, but for now, here is the outline.

Step One

Acknowledge the failure and formally address it with the Ministry Leader.

Accept responsibility, but clearly identify the failure. This is known as grace! However, the Ministry Leader is given notice that they have entered the first phase of discipline. Along with the acknowledgement, corrective action or training is implemented and everything is documented.

Step Two

If Step One does not correct the failure, then the burden of restoration falls on the Ministry Leader.

A performance agreement is put in place to measure specific corrective actions or behaviors of the Ministry Leader over a specified period of time. This agreement is signed by both the Staff Leader and Ministry Leader. The specified time parameter passes, and measurements are taken.

Step Three

If Step Two does not restore the Ministry Leader to successful performance, then reassignment or termination is agreed upon. Reassignment takes place for any volunteer; and can occur for paid Ministry Leaders with exceptional value to the Organization.

Staff Leaders Are Decision-Makers And Communicators.

Another exceptional quality of Staff Leaders is that they understand the nuances of decision-making. Ministry Leaders work in their areas of responsibility with the authority to make decisions within the confines of the pursuit of the Six Love Languages and their established plans and budgets in the Master Plan. However, from time-to-time gray areas will arise, such as a special event the time and place of which may affect other ministries, a new idea or curriculum which may need to be incorporated into a ministry, or a new group of volunteers may need to be recruited which may affect other ministries. A Staff Leader may need to get involved in these kinds of decisions, not to direct the Ministry Leader, but to assist him or her.

Staff Leaders Understand Three Levels Of Assisting Others With Decisions In These Kinds Of Gray Areas.

Level One

The simplest decisions to make are those that merely need to be communicated to a ministry group without input from other Ministry Leaders. Communication is always necessary for all those affected by decisions, but some are simple enough that input from others is unnecessary. Staff Leaders have the maturity to know when they are faced with this kind of decision.

Level Two

When bringing together a group of Ministry Leaders, it is necessary to weigh the effects of a decision. There are times when a Ministry Leader's decision is going to affect another ministry. In those cases, the other Ministry Leader should be included in the decision-making process. The Staff Leader understands this nuance and assists by bringing together the parts of the team affected for a collaborative decision.

Level Three

When a decision will have far reaching effects, will create sufficient change in the Organization's methods or approaches to speaking one or more of the Love Languages, may require remodeling or adding spaces to the building, or may require a large capital expense, the Staff Leader needs to be able to implement a process of planting and watering the decision. Large scale decisions like these need time to germinate in the Organization. The Staff Leader will walk the Ministry Leader through the timing of allowing his or her thoughts to be planted with the Executive Team, the Staff Leadership team, the Ministry Leader team, and the entire Organization before making a decision of this magnitude.

Staff Leaders Are Good At Working With Teams.

Staff Leaders need to be able to employ good group dynamics skills when they collaborate with each other. As we have seen, the Staff Leader function is rarely performed by one person at a time. In any size church, there will undoubtedly be needs for Staff Leaders to work together. In the Skills Typically Not Taught chapter in the functionality section of this book, (See Chapter 14, Page 229) skills are outlined for when Staff Leaders work with each other.

It is critical to understand that The Boss is ever-present. The conversations and discussions of these leaders need to please Him at every turn in content, tone, character, and consensus.

Staff Leaders Act As Resources For The Executive Team.

Another role Staff Leaders perform for the Organization is to act as consultants to the Executive Team. (See Chapter 6, Page 89) Staff Leaders meet with the Executive Team at their request to work on two things.

- Getting answers to their questions
- Creating solutions for the problems they face

This may mean gathering data or investigating the thoughts of Ministry Leaders or their teams. It may mean inventing new processes, creating new methods, or suggesting alternatives. Staff Leaders take the lead in such endeavors. They do the research, discover solutions that other churches may be utilizing, talk to colleagues, draw work-flow diagrams, use quality tools, and form problem-solving teams where necessary. They do not allow the Executive Team to struggle with finding solutions for the problems that arise. This means they do NOT take problems TO the Executive Team. Instead, they find solutions FOR them, and if the Executive Team does not like a particular solution, the Staff Leader will find another for them.

Staff Leaders Are Trainers.

One final role the Staff Leader performs for the Organization is as a corporate trainer. It amazes me how little training goes on in the church. You can find group after group that will teach you the Bible or connect you with other Christians in like stages of life; however, typically, if a Ministry Leader struggles with effectiveness, the Organization reacts more to why the leader was hired or placed in the role rather than ever having thoughts about providing them with training.

Staff Leaders are always on the watch for opportunities to train Ministry Leaders to be more successful. Many of the skills not typically taught will be discussed in the functionality section of this book. (See Chapter 14, Page 229) Staff Leaders see weaknesses and ineffectiveness as opportunities for growth long before seeing them as failures in need of discipline. They are trainers by instinct!

CHAPTER 6
The Executive Team

In the typical congregation, the Executive Team is made up of its elders, but not in every case. Other groups can comprise the Executive Team.

- Representatives of cross-sectional demographic groups
- A small sub-group of the elders
- Larger groups of elders, deacons, and trustees
- A small group of paid staff and congregational leaders with executive experience

In most cases, this team is formed to expedite decision-making that typically falls on this group; therefore, it is typically held to a small representative number that can function with fewer inputs and obstacles. In many churches, this group is formed for maximum command and control for the Organization, which runs contrary to its fundamental purpose in the management structure proposed in this book.

The role of the Executive Team should answer one question on behalf of the Organization. Are we healthy? As with every other layer of the Org Chart, the Executive Team can only claim success if all the layers above it are succeeding at speaking the Six Love Languages to which The Boss's ear is inclined. Their first line of watch care and most immediate concern is for the success of the Staff Leaders serving directly above them. They also sit at the bottom of the chart looking upward through all the layers looking for well-being on every layer above them. Their burning question remains, "Are we healthy?" No matter how your church comprises its Executive Team, its role and function as the bottom layer of management in our Org Chart is clear and its attributes are clearly identifiable.

It is important at this point to re-establish the premise of this book as one about an effective management structure for the Organization we know as the church. The church's history is fraught with failure when any structure is introduced that places human authority between God and His church. In many contemporary churches, leaders (or would-be leaders) have used two verses of scripture to seize control of everything going on in the Organization: Titus 1:7 and 1 Timothy 5:17.

The term "manages" or "directs" in each verse is used to place the elders of the church in complete control. If the image from scripture is a human body, and Christ is the Head, these people want to be the neck. If the picture is a kingdom and Christ is the King, they want to be the princes or governors. If the picture is a flock, and Christ is the Good Shepherd, they want to be the collie dog. If the picture is a family and God is the Father, they want what Joseph had in Potiphar's house. Control!

I have already laid out the case for God as The Boss of His Organization, as well as His capacity to function in that role by being the controlling influence in the heart of each of His followers. Rare are the historical instances that the church has thrived in its disciple-making commission when human authority has been positioned between God and His church. It's a mistake to allow any person to think they can manage or direct the affairs of the church better than, or instead of, God on any level or in any manner.

What we have lacked is trust in The Boss, adherence to His clearly established principles and goals for the church, and a management structure that can handle the day-by-day operation of the Organization without deposing Him. In this light, let's look at the role of the Executive Team on our chart.

Spiritual Leaders by Example

1 Peter 5:1-4 gives a clear picture of the kind of functionality that exists in the Executive Team. The pagan religious culture surrounding the first century church was filled with priests and priestesses who controlled the worshipers in their temples with rules and rituals. They arbitrated the kinds of acceptable worship and sacrifice their gods expected from the people. While doing so, they were involved in all kinds of corrupt behavior and filled with greed.

In response, Peter tells the elders of the church they were to lead in complete contrast to the management structures found in these pagan temples. They were to lead by example, watching over their churches like shepherds watch over sheep. They were not to become the kinds of overlords they so easily observed among the pagans.

The first function of the Executive Team in our management structure is to demonstrate such spiritual maturity that every member of the Organization would aspire to live like them. That quality of lifestyle is a prerequisite to all the other functions of the Executive Team.

Being a spiritual example of the Holy Spirit's control means giving priority to Him in everything. Colossians 3 says we can actually do everything we do, whether in word or deed, in the name of Jesus. Members of the Executive Team master this level of spirituality and exemplify it to the Organization.

The vast majority of everything Paul writes to Timothy and Titus regarding attributes that qualify a person to be an elder are about spirituality. It amazes me how often I've seen elders, meeting behind closed doors, abandon the character traits that qualified them to be meeting in those rooms. Anger, self-promotion, control issues, and pride surface so quickly that it's shocking.

In every meeting of the Executive Team, there should be two agreed-upon standing operating guidelines.

- Everyone on the team should place themselves in accountability to everyone else in the room in terms of temperament and conduct and should be willing to be called out for outbursts that betray their submission to the Holy Spirit's control. There should exist such commitment to The Boss and trust in each other that everyone in the room would humbly accept correction from the others.

- There should be such an awareness of the presence of The Boss at every meeting of the Executive Team that its members would willingly suspend any discussion that prohibited them from speaking love to Him. If either the content of the discussion or its tone would in any way embarrass The Boss, then everyone should agree to suspend it, stop the meeting, walk away, and table the topic, maybe permanently. If discussing it outside the parameters of love for The Boss seems necessary, it would be better to call the topic unnecessary. The Executive Team should be so bound by its calling to leadership that its members would be reviled by any such discussion. Leading by example means that spiritual maturity comes first!

The Executive Team should live by this code: *We will not ask this Organization to live at a higher level of spiritual conduct than we do.*

This quality of leadership by example, extends outside the meeting room for this team. The Executive Team should demonstrate such a commitment to The Boss, to the Organization, and to each other that their marriages, families, co-workers, friends, and even Sunday visitors notice how well they live in step with the Holy Spirit. This team should live by the axiom that more is caught than taught. They should understand that the credibility to serve on the Executive Team is earned by a lifestyle that speaks love to The Boss in every facet of life.

There is another key means by which the Executive Team gets its credibility with the Organization. They know the Six Love Languages and speak them fluently! My experience with leadership teams leads me to understand that most of the time they would like to fulfill their perceived role as overseers by merely watching the congregation speak these languages. They think an overseer leads by observation.

The truth is that the congregation watches the Executive Team much more than the Executive Team watches the congregation. If the Executive Team members are always found observing the Organization, the members of the Organization learn a terrible lesson, which is that spiritually mature people watch what's going on when the church speaks love to God. The concept that spiritual maturity means spectating is a terrible lesson that can only be overcome by the Executive Team.

- When the church speaks the Language of Adoration, the Executive Team speaks it with them. They speak it genuinely, passionately, and openly in spirit and truth. They lead by example. In fact, they speak the Language of Adoration so well that they cannot keep from speaking it when in corporate worship with the Organization.
- Members of the Executive Team demonstrate the difference Jesus makes in the life of a disciple because the transformation He is making in their lives is so evident. The Word of God and the guid-

ance of the Holy Spirit are actively at work in them. The words of my mouth and the meditations of my heart are pleasing to you, my Rock and my Redeemer! (Psalm 19:14) They speak the Love Language of Transformation!

- The Executive Team treats everyone in the church with the "One Anothers" of scripture as models of what it means to be true companions of those in the Organization knowing how to fulfill the command of The Boss to love one another.

- The Executive Team members are humble people, who continuously show compassion to hurting people, unable to ignore anyone who is weak, fallen, helpless, hopeless, or destitute. They speak the Language of Compassion as Jesus did.

- You will always find members of the Executive Team partnering with God to advance His kingdom's ideals and goals. They give. They invest. They know their gifts and partner with The Boss for the good of the church speaking the Language of Partnership in a way that makes others want to invest, too.

- The Executive Team members are the most passionate about evangelism, the mission of making disciples. They know how to talk to people about Jesus and do so constantly because they are committed to evangelism. They fall asleep praying about it, wake up thinking about it, and take advantage of every opportunity they find to express the Language of evangelism.

One final attribute helps define the role of the Executive Team. They are good at absorbing slings and arrows. They understand the concept of putting up with the failings of the weak, even as they submit to the leadership of The Boss. There are times when this is a difficult task, but these spiritually mature people will handle it well. When members of the Organization come to them with their issues, Executive Team members are able to discern the difference between real issues and mere complaints, which typically come from people who are speaking about things they simply dislike.

Executive Team members know when they are hearing complaints and handle them with grace and understanding while remaining undeterred in their pursuit of the goals laid out by The Boss. They recognize when comments from the Organization represent real issues regarding the speaking of the Six Love Languages. Comments like these are important to the health of the Organization and should be brought to the rest of the Executive Team for prayerful consideration.

Roles as Shepherds

Shepherds understand that you can't MANAGE sheep! The book, *They Smell Like Sheep* by Dr. Lynn Anderson would make an excellent study for this attribute of the Executive Team. The leadership role as a shepherd demands that members of the Executive Team ask the same questions about their flock as a real shepherd asks about his. Are we healthy? Is everybody together? Has anyone wondered off? Is anyone sick? Does someone need special attention? Is anyone feeling alone? Are there any threats to the flock? Is everyone safe? Can we reach good pastures tomorrow? Will the flock have water to drink in the morning?

Questions like these dominate the time, energy, and discussions of the Executive Team. In this case, it's not the thought that counts, like it might be with a Christmas or birthday gift. Caring is like praise. If it exists only in your head, it doesn't really exist at all. It must be expressed to be real. The Executive Team cannot sit in a board room reading reports about the health of the flock and fulfill their obligation to this role of leadership in the Organization.

They must be out with the sheep, in among the sheep, letting the sheep hear their voice and feel their touch. Sheep won't follow a voice they've never heard, in fact, they run from it. Whatever the size of the congregation, the Executive Team members must know their flock. The people they serve should hear their words of encouragement, feel their handshakes, see their smiles, receive cups of cold water from them from time to time, and on some occasions have their feet washed by them. This may be a foreign concept to many contemporary church's Executive Teams as it reflects a management structure that to them has long since outlived its usefulness.

Thoughts like these come from the belief that Executive Teams exist to manage and control the Organizations they serve. Since sheep can neither be managed nor controlled, this creates frustration for Executive Teams causing many to change both their fundamental purpose and functionality.

It comes back to trusting in the Chief Shepherd as the manager and controller of the Organization. The Executive Team must believe that The Boss knows how to exert control when it's necessary. He knows what He wants from the Organization and He wants His Executive Team to trust Him. Leading by example demonstrates trust in The Boss. Leading by trying to control the Organization, does not.

Roles as Overseers

It may be a struggle to imagine how Executive Team members can oversee an Organization from the bottom layer of the Org Chart. Maybe "underseer" is a better term for this role. Even though they see themselves in the bottom layer of the chart, they should view the entire Organization from that perspective, and they do so without a thought of controlling it. With wise eyes they watch for specific signs of health, and they are given the tools to do just that. If Executive Team members find signs of weakness or ill health in the Organization, their instinctive reaction is to talk to The Boss about it! This group fasts, prays, and seeks the face of The Boss with regularity. They understand, as Moses did in the wilderness, that if the cloud has moved, it's time for the people to move with it. When there's not enough to eat or drink, it's time to head to the Tent of Meeting and talk to The Boss! Their desire to please The Boss and follow His lead is so strong, they can think of no other response to anything in the Organization needing their attention.

Performing the role of overseers requires that the Executive Team members have specific tools or points or reference from which to gain their insights.

- They use the Six Love Languages as measurements. The functionality section of this book details how to measure the health of the Organization by the strength of the Six Love Languages. For now, understand that it is the role of the Executive Team to keep their eyes on these six qualities in the church they undersee. They watch, listen, observe behaviors, and sense in their spirits the positive effects of these languages.

They also take careful note of anything contrary to them, such as characteristics from the lists in Colossians 3 like impurity, lust, evil desires, greed, anger, rage, malice, slander, and filthy language. They know the differences between health and sickness in the Organization and are quick to recognize those differences.

There are Spirit-led responses to both the positive and negative influences the Executive Team finds while underseeing the Organization. These will be outlined in the next section of this book, but for now take caution. It is not the Executive Team's responsibility to attempt to correct every weakness they find. The members of this team have a prerequisite firmly in place that protects them from poor responses because their temperament and conduct are fully submitted to the control of The Boss! They use whatever they find while watching for the Six Love Languages (or lack thereof) to help them recognize and clarify the needs of the Organization.

The kinds of corrections that may come to mind most quickly can lead to the worst kinds of responses an Executive Team might make when finding weaknesses among the people in the Organization. The Holy Spirit is quite capable of making corrections in people's behavior when they need it. The Executive Team must always remember who The Boss is when it comes to correcting people. There are occasions when this group may gently approach a person trapped in a lifestyle sin for the sake of restoration, but only as shepherds of his or her soul.

- They use the Master Plan! The Executive Team should never find itself asking evangelism, "What's going on?" The Executive Team is responsible for assembling the Master Plan, which is the document that informs the whole Organization of The Boss's plan year by year. Every Ministry Leader in the Organization is responsible for answering seven questions yearly about the functionality of their ministries. When compiled, their answers form the Master Plan for the Organization. The Executive Team oversees this process, therefore, they ALWAYS know what is going on, because once assembled, everyone adheres to the plan!

  As they assemble the Master Plan, the Executive Team has the opportunity to discover what The Boss has in mind for the Organization. This process provides an opportunity to watch for weaknesses in the plan while measuring it against the Six Love Languages as they ask several questions. (Is there enough Adoration in our plan? Do we plan to speak the language of Evangelism sufficiently this year? Are we offering hurting people real help? Will the "One Anothers" be spoken by our people this year?) What is their response if they find weaknesses in the Master Plan? TALK TO THE BOSS!!! (and inform the Organization)

To be guided by the gifting of The Boss means that the Executive Team believes that the capacity to accomplish everything The Boss desires in a given year, He has also gifted into the Organization. If the Executive Team finds weakness in the Master Plan in one or more of the Six Love Languages, it means that there are people in the Organization with unused gifts. It's time for The Boss to awaken them regarding their abilities and time for the Organization to join with the Executive Team in talking with The Boss about those gifts. "Wake up, oh sleeper, and arise from the dead; Christ is going to shine on you!!"

If, after talking to The Boss for a period of time, the Executive Team determines that there remains a functional hole in the Organization, particularly in a mission critical area of functionality, it may be time to pursue a Ministry Leader with special skill or experience to help the Organization. The Executive Team determines this while keeping the church informed.

- They use their Staff Leaders as consultants! Way too often the elders, or Executive Team of a church find themselves trying to solve problems. They may discuss problems that exist in the Organization for months, thinking it's their responsibility to be a problem-solving group. I cannot overstate the tremendous obstacle and mountainous dysfunctionality this mentality presents to the Organization. In any corporation, it's not those in the bottom layers of the Organization that are tasked with solving the problems for the top layers. It's the top layers that are supposed to present the Organization with solutions to problems that will enable the Organization to more easily accomplish its goals.

The Executive Team needs to become good at recognizing when they have devolved into problem-solving discussions and at those points, call in their Staff Leader consultants. The Executive Team hands any given problem to these leaders who find the appropriate people to become problem-solving teams to find solutions and bring them to the Executive Team for inclusion in the Master Plan.

Staying Informed about the Organization

If certain points are true about Executive Team members, then staying informed about the Organization is a relatively simple task.

- The Executive Team members know the Six Love Languages and speak them fluently.
- After assembling the Master Plan, the Executive Team members read and understand it thoroughly.
- As shepherds, the members of the Executive Team are in constant contact with the Organization.

Meetings of the Executive Team are characterized by the following components.

1. Inputs are shared concerning the Organization regarding specific or special needs arising within it (i.e., someone's house just burned down, an individual is on death's doorstep, a call was received from a member requesting anointing and prayer, a ministry just had a great success or failure, a small group has raised a concern about their ability to speak one of the Six Love Languages).
2. Feedback is received from Staff Leaders regarding progress or use of the Master Plan (i.e., ongoing results from existing ministries, results from a special effort undertaken by the Organization, solutions to problems as tasked to them by the Executive Team, specific unexpected consequences observed while implementing the Master Plan either positive or negative).
3. Concern is expressed by the team regarding the spiritual health of its members (i.e., extra heavy burdens being born, families of team members enduring hardships, persecutions from outside the Organization affecting one or more of the members, burnout, exhaustion or discouragement being endured by the members of the team).
4. Consideration for the health of the Organization based on the Six Love Languages is shared (i.e., times of fasting and prayer, comments based on observed successes or failures, worship, fellowship, or evangelistic results).

The concern of the Executive Team is always for the health of the Organization. Discussions of other subjects are reserved for other times and places. A good practice for this group is to routinely ask Ministry Leaders to meet with the team for prayer and support. This request must be appropriately couched in comfort, support, and encouragement, never criticism or complaint. This is a good way for the Executive Team to note first-hand the spiritual fervor in the congregation.

PART 2:
THE FUNCTIONALITY

Most corporate leaders know you can describe a company with organizational charts which explain roles and relationships, but success results from what is happening in the spaces between the layers of the chart. It's the functionality that makes or breaks the organization. These are often intangible factors like culture, morale, communication, and innovation. Are new ideas considered or quashed? Are small victories celebrated or ignored? Do employees feel free to openly express their concerns or are they made to feel better off by hiding them?

Other times the functional factors affecting success are more objective. Does everyone know the mission of the Organization? Is everyone driven by the same set of operational principles? Is there a plan to which everyone contributes and does each person understand how their work affects the plan?

A third set of factors comes from within each worker. Does each employee feel that they are working in their area of expertise with their developed skill set? Are expectations and areas of responsibility clear to each individual?

Critical Factors About the Principles of Functionality

These factors and the answers to these questions are just as critical to the success of the church as they are in business because the answers outline the functionality of the Organization. For the church to succeed, a culture must be built around specific principles.

The Master Plan

The adage, "if you fail to plan then you are planning to fail" holds a lot of truth. If The Boss is going to manage the Organization directly through His presence in the heart of every member and if Ministry Leaders are going to provide the Organization with opportunities to speak love to Him, then the thoughts of those top-level folks are going to have to be easy to observe.

If everyone in the top layer of the Organization feels free to follow the leading of The Boss without letting everyone else know where they are going, chaos will result, thus, the reason and need for a Master Plan. It is necessary not only to put a plan together, but to teach everyone to work within the parameters of the plan after it's assembled.

The Master Plan provides everyone in the church with all the information they need to know about the cumulative applied efforts of the Organization in any given year.

- It becomes The Boss's control document for the Organization. It allows for cross-checking the duplication of efforts.

- It creates opportunities for cooperation and collaboration.
- Once assembled, everyone sticks with it! If a crisis, or a special opportunity arises during any given year, the plan can be adjusted on the fly; however, every layer of the Organization must have input to these changes, and communication with the total membership must be ample in such cases. (i.e., a pandemic strikes!)

The Objectives

For the functionality to be powerful and effective, everyone in the Organization must be pulling in the same direction. Everyone must see the accomplishment of the same set of goals as their collective mission. Everyone must believe that speaking the Six Love Languages to The Boss will please Him and create success for the Organization. Every individual Ministry Leader must see how their efforts will bond with the efforts of all the other Ministry Leaders to form a comprehensive effort to please The Boss.

These never change. Measurements will be created for these languages, which will determine success criteria for the whole Organization. The Six Love Languages must be taught to the whole Organization and form the basis for success in the conversations of every layer of it.It is also critical to see that in every moment the church spends achieving its objectives, the people's temperament and conduct must exhibit The Boss's control. It is impossible to think that while speaking love to God, any member of the Organization would conduct himself or herself outside the parameters of the fruits of the Spirit. Therefore, everything said and done must be tempered with love, joy, peace, patience, kindness, goodness, faithfulness, gentleness, and self-control. Any group that functions in the context of accomplishing the objectives of the church must dismiss or disband if it routinely operates outside these parameters, because, by definition, their meetings are not pleasing to The Boss.

Clarified Responsibilities

Every Ministry Leader in the Organization, by virtue of the Master Planning process, clearly identifies the areas of responsibility in which they will function. This clarification should never be construed as an effort to create silo effects or turf for their ministries but is done specifically to outline areas of concentration for collaboration and cooperation with other ministries. Responsibilities are different from objectives, tasks, or job descriptions.

Giving someone responsibility over a demographic portion of a congregation or over a specific love language, leaves room for The Boss to speak, inspire, and control the planning and outcomes of a ministry. This responsibility also creates an urgency and passion in Ministry Leaders who recognize that a portion of the success of the church lies with them. Clarified responsibilities are better than detailed job descriptions for Ministry Leaders.

Giftedness

When Ministry Leaders function in the areas of their gift-edness several powerful things happen.

- They make deeper connections with The Boss who gifted them.
- They are more contented with their work knowing that they are fulfilling their personal purpose in the Organization.
- Their sense of belonging and worth to everyone else who is functioning alongside them increases, according to Romans 12.
- Their awareness of the giftedness and value of everyone functioning differently than they are increases.
- They recognize the love that binds everyone together as the body of Christ is built up as each part does its work.

By operating in their area of their gifts, Ministry Leaders help shape the ministry direction of the church. The church often gets into a habit or rut of thinking that the existing ministries define God's direction for the church. In these cases, programs define ministry efforts and change becomes difficult, if not impossible. People are told to complete gift assessments in order for programming directors to find boxes where the people best fit.

When a church allows the gifts of its people to define the direction of its ministry, The Boss is in full control of where it goes, how it changes, and how success will be defined. When existing programming defines a ministry, people are coerced into roles and a status quo is developed that over time confines or overrides the will of the Spirit and the control of The Boss.

Working for The Boss

All the Ministry Leaders in the Organization work to please The Boss and are responsive to His direction. Left to please themselves, their Staff Leaders, or their Executive Team, their self-motivated efforts will soon fail. However, if their motivation is to please God, that motivation will never wane. The Organization will always be staffed by volunteers. Volunteers must see their work as their efforts to respond to God's investment in them.

Jesus was never shy about analogizing God with a landowner, vineyard owner, or a wealthy investor. In each role God, commissions workers expecting them to produce results with His investment in them. All people, and especially all Ministry Leaders, in the church need to see how their work is connected to the pleasure of The Boss, and that connection must be relied upon as the motivation for their work.

This should be good news for a host of tired Ministry Leaders who feel the need to constantly cheerlead and tangibly reward their volunteers just to keep them motivated.

Church leaders have shied away from talking about working to please God for to keep people from thinking they can earn their salvation by their works, which they cannot. As a result, people have been made to feel as though they are working to please church leaders rather than God. People don't do their best work when they try to please people.

They do their best work when they try to please the One who saved them, not so that He WILL save them, but because He ALREADY HAS!

Ministry Leaders who are best at pleasing The Boss have character traits, which are necessary for the church to succeed with the proposed management system.

- **Ministry Leaders are independent thinkers.**
  They think in macro terms and plan in micro terms, assuming responsibility for their areas of ministry with a view to giving people their best opportunity to speak one or more of the Six Love Languages.

- **Ministry Leaders are collaborative by nature.**
  They know they don't function in a vacuum, but in concert with others who are helping in the overall effort to please The Boss. They are communicative, courteous, and cooperative with others, as well as flexible when necessary.

- **Ministry Leaders believe in excellence.**
  They do nothing half-heartedly, believing that if anything is worth doing, it is worth doing well. Understanding that success breeds success, and mediocrity more mediocrity, they limit what they do to the efforts that can receive sufficient attention and will reflect their standard of excellence.

- **Ministry Leaders are humble.**
  They have submitted themselves so fully to the control

of the Holy Spirit that their egos are no longer connected to their work. The praise they receive from others in the Organization does not puff them up. They are quick to compliment others and realistic about what they hear about themselves looking at themselves with sober judgment. (Romans 12)

- **Ministry Leaders are innovators.**
  They know when programming has become stale or ineffective and are proactive about finding and using other means to accomplish better results. They do not fear change but recognize and embrace change when it is necessary.

Leaders who Trust The Boss

Leaders who see that God has gifted His church with the abilities to accomplish what He wants done are most open to following Him anywhere He wants to go. Leaders whose trust is in their own vision for the Organization will hinder it. It is critical for leaders to see that God knows what He is doing, and if He wants something else to be done, He will supply what is needed to accomplish it. This applies to every layer of the Organizational chart and affects everything that is planned and accomplished by the work of the church. Therefore, God receives the glory for everything that succeeds!

It is only when this factor is in place that the Executive Team can humbly evaluate the health of the Organization and have the good sense to talk to The Boss when they find weaknesses in it.

CHAPTER 7
People Management and Discipline

It is interesting, if not tragic, that the paid staff in many churches are treated more poorly than many employees in the corporate world. Corporate leaders are instructed by human resource managers concerning the substantial negative consequences that result from treating employees less than fairly. Church leaders should be taught more about this. It is baffling that those who spiritually qualify to lead in the church can so quickly and easily, when managing people, depart from the temperament and conduct that qualified them to lead.

It is even more interesting and more tragic that those same staff members must in turn treat their volunteers far better than they are treated by their supervisors and church leaders. Seldom are they able to learn skills and techniques that generate and encourage a desire to succeed or excel. Their personal experiences with those who supervise them do not teach them the skills they need even though they should be their older spiritual brothers. There seems to be a tremendous lack of understanding and training in people management skills in the ministry preparation curriculum of our Staff Leaders.

In addition to this weakness, the church historically has lacked a fair, but firm, way of applying discipline to staff members who demonstrate the need for it because there seems to be no standardized method for dealing with those failures. When undergoing discipline, staff members are consistently caught off guard since there is no established method or policy in place. If they are treated differently from one another, they have no way to clearly understand the process by which they are being either restored or terminated. When no consistent standard is applied to everyone equally, staff members routinely feel unjustifiably singled out as others don't seem to be disciplined in similar ways for similar failures. Disciplinary inequity is death to the morale of any group of employees.

It is imperative that the church manage its Ministry Leaders in ways that keep them motivated by The Boss to do their best work. When discipline is required, everyone is treated fairly and similarly with the same process.

These people management principles were listed and explained earlier in this book. In this section on functionality, I will explain how and why these principles work.

Temperament and Conduct

A standard that must be established, expected, and maintained when managing people in the church demonstrates nothing less than appropriate temperament and conduct. This means that in every interaction of Ministry Leaders, Staff Leaders and Executive Team Members with anyone else in the Organization there must be a commitment to allow The Boss, the Holy Spirit, to produce His fruit. Galatians 5 lists them as love, joy, peace, patience, kindness, goodness, faithfulness, gentleness, and self-control.

These must be agreed upon as the accepted standard of excellence to which everyone adheres when dealing with each other in the process of working in the church. Failure to adhere must be addressed as an opportunity to improve until or unless resistance to conformity necessitates discipline. The members of the Organization can never be expected to treat each other better than the standard set by their leaders.

What this action produces is a bond of unity in the Spirit, creating a safe environment for collaboration and cooperation. It demonstrates the constant presence of The Boss as He presides over every interaction of people in His Organization assuring that any discussion will not devolve into a quarrelsome argument. It allows everyone to speak the truth in love, without leaving out the love! As this standard works its way into the Organization, an atmosphere of trust develops, and the church becomes a safe place for any person to open their heart to any leader in it.

This principle works as well downward as it does upward through the Org Chart. It is not a principle for particular roles in particular layers of the chart but should be taught to and expected by every member of the Organization. Galatians 5 also tells us that if we would live by the Spirit, we must keep in step with the Spirit. It is not optional or occasionally that we do this, it is the constant expectation of The Boss!

Four Principles of People Management

Care

When Ministry Leaders care about the person doing the work more than they care about the work they produce, that person becomes more productive. It is amazing that in the church, people who manage people think that they can once and for all, inform and train those with whom they work and on some indefinite ongoing basis, they'll give their best efforts toward completing that work. That may happen by some spiritually humble and enduringly patient person, but it should not be expected and can never become the norm. The first guiding principle of people management in the church is that caring produces more caring.

How is this demonstrated? If you manage people either as a Ministry Leader, Staff Leader, or Executive Team member, you should know the answers to these questions and your answers should not be an embarrassment to you.

Do you know the names of the family members of everyone with whom you work? How much more intimate do you believe your prayers for this person would be if you did? How much more personal would your interest be in their battles and victories if you knew every family member of those with whom you work?

When was the last time you knelt beside the desk or in the living room of those with whom you work to let them listen to you pray exclusively for them (not the missionaries of your church, those on the sick list, the church staff or elders, but just them) and their family? What do you think would happen to their attention to you and the work they produce if they heard you praying for them and the ones they love with personal interest and concern?

How often have you offered those with whom you work extra time to attend to personal issues when you know they will fulfill their responsibilities at other times and in other ways? Do you ever give the gift of trust to your people?

How do you treat people in their moments of failure? Do you help them see their failures as opportunities to improve as a result, or are you quick to point to their failures as an immediate need for correction and possible discipline?

Are your compliments for good work ever accompanied by small yet tangible rewards? Do the people with whom you work ever get more than an "atta boy" for their successes?

Demonstrations of concern for people cannot only be thoughts expressed in text messages, emails, or phone calls. Caring demands action to be real! When you manage people in the church, whether it be upward or downward on the Org Chart, they need to know first how much you care for them.

Eliminate Obstacles

There are very few people who attempt tasks planning to be unsuccessful. People want to succeed. Some of the worst conditions in which to place workers are ones where their expectations are unclear, where their process has known bottlenecks in it, and where they will meet with resistance when they need to collaborate or interface with others while attempting to succeed. The second guiding principle in people management is to continuously offer people an unencumbered pathway to success by eliminating any obstacles that would hinder them.

Good supervisors must develop a conscience that bothers them when they are uncertain about what may be hindering their workers from performing at their best. In fact, before starting their own work, any Ministry Leader or Staff Leader should be uncomfortable until they are certain that everyone working for them can be completely successful with their daily work. It is simply unconscionable to leave others without everything they need to succeed if it is in your power to eliminate their obstacles for them.

Be advised that eliminating obstacles does not mean doing someone's work for them, nor does it mean enabling them to continue practices that are ineffective. It means that if any worker is consistently running into the same roadblocks in their work, you will become actively involved in helping remove them. Doing this creates a team environment where workers thrive. A good question to learn to ask is, "Is there anything keeping you from being 100% effective today?"

Balance the Load

The easiest and most effective solution to the problem of getting work done in the church is to find passionate people with reasonable skills and load the work on them, that is, until they break down under the burden. Good people with good attitudes and above average skills find it hard to say no to those who ask them to work for the church. Good singers are asked to sing…a lot. Good teachers are asked to teach…a lot. Good children's workers are asked to work with kids…a lot. As it is often noted, "80% of the work gets done by 20% of the people."

It is incumbent on someone who is tracking both the workers and the workload that the load is balanced. One of the greatest tragedies in the church is to see people lose their fundamental faith because of the pressures brought on not by persecutions or trials in the world around them, but by church programming. Overburdened and burned out, they question their moorings with Christ. Sometimes, they make tragic choices to leave not only their churches, but husbands or wives, jobs, or worst of all…their children. Unfortunately, the root cause is that the church has not carefully watched over their spiritual well-being, but has, instead, heaped responsibility on them until they break down under the load.

When managing people in the church, Ministry Leaders, Staff Leaders and Executive Team members must carefully consider how much of the programming load is being carried by every involved person in the Organization. This takes vigilance, demanding a constant watch over those who are functioning in the Body and requiring sensitivity to the personal needs of people. People can never become warm bodies filling gaps or holes in programs.

These questions should be asked. How thinly are you spread in your work life? How well is your family responding to your involvement at church? Do you feel engaged and passionate about what you are doing for God in the church? Is the church feeding and ministering to you well?

Provide Feedback

People want to know how they are doing at whatever they are attempting to do by those who know the most about it. When a professional golfer stands on a practice tee hitting golf balls, that person does not want a swing coach standing behind them simply admiring every shot they hit. Many golfers have switched to getting their feedback from cameras and computers, which give them accurate, precise information after every shot. People who work in the church deserve the same consideration.

Feedback typically comes in two forms and church leaders have been notoriously weak at both.

- **Positive Reinforcement and Compliments**
  It's not that leaders haven't complimented the people they are leading, but that the compliments are distant and detached from the work. Telling a Ministry Leader that they have done a good job in a casual, off-handed way tells them more about what you do not understand about their work than it communicates praise for it.

For positive reinforcement to connect with a worker it must be timely, specific, and demonstrate a real comprehension of what has been accomplished. When I preach a sermon and people tell me, "Nice sermon, preacher," it does very little to encourage me. When they say, "I will be thinking about what you said about this specific issue" or "the Holy Spirit went to work on me when you were explaining this scripture," I am greatly encouraged!

- **Negative Feedback and Criticism**

    When delivering negative feedback, care must be given to allow for self- examination by the worker. They should not be made to feel that someone is criticizing or critiquing them, but rather that someone is investigating a failure with which they are ready to help. The best approach is to start with questions like, "How do you think that went? Did it accomplish what you wanted it to accomplish? Do you think you planned well and had sufficient resources to achieve the goal you set?"

    Allowing a worker to assess their own failures is far superior to telling them about them. Spirit-led people will want to know when they fail! Not addressing failure is detrimental in three ways.

    » The worker does not know how to improve.

» Those working with the person who is failing come to realize that their own failures will never be addressed.

» It is not enjoyable to work in a system that makes no corrections when the people working in it fail.

In summary, and before proceeding with the disciplinary plan, it is critical to implement these people management principles with all Ministry Leaders, Staff Leaders, and Executive Team Members in the Organization. Everyone must be aware of the principles by which they are being managed before any discipline is applied to them. Only when people see and feel the effects of these principles will they be prepared to be disciplined. When these principles are established, if or when discipline becomes necessary, it will never come as a surprise.

Three-Step Discipline Plan

As previously explained, a method needs to exist in the church to address performance failure. In this section, we will review the three steps and explain the effectiveness of handling discipline with a specific plan.

Before we begin, if there are policies for termination that will not be handled with discipline, they must be made clear to everyone working in the Organization. Here are a few examples.

- If your church has a firearms policy prohibiting firearms in the building during business hours, it must be in compliance with and posted as directed by the laws of your state. When that policy is violated, the person violating it can and should be terminated without going through the three-step discipline plan.
- If your church has an internet policy prohibiting people from using church computers to watch or download pornography, any person doing so in violation of that policy can and should be terminated without going through the three-step discipline plan.
- If your church runs background checks on its children's workers and someone working for the Organization in the children's ministry is found later to have a history of child molestation, they can and should be removed from that ministry without going through the three-step discipline plan.
- Other causes for termination and/or removal might include (among others) embezzlement, sexual promiscuity, misuse of church funds, vandalism of church property, inappropriate counseling advice, or substance abuse. Obviously, any policy relating to these or other issues would need to be in compliance with local laws and terms of insurance policies.

There are causes for which removal from a church ministry can and should be exercised without discipline. It is important that everyone working in the Organization understand these causes and the policies that will remove them from service without undergoing discipline. Many ugly situations in which churches have found themselves could have been avoided if behaviors mandating immediate removal were clearly stated in policies and taught to the workers.

Functionality of the Three-Step Discipline Plan

Discipline of employees or workers in the church should never come as a surprise. If the principles of people management have been applied and are commonly used with those working in the Organization, then areas of failure should have been identified and discussed long before discipline is required. There will, however, be times or cases in which an employee or worker must undergo discipline. It is critical that anyone undergoing discipline knows that there are two completely different outcomes that can result from the process. One is complete restoration, and the other is termination or removal.

The church must maintain a balance between acknowledged failure and grace. There must be an offering of complete restoration even as discipline is applied; therefore, whomever is shepherding or overseeing the Ministry Leader, Staff Leader or Executive Team Member requiring discipline must make it clear that the person needing discipline has entered the discipline plan.

Step One

The person responsible for oversight of the worker needing discipline assumes full responsibility for their failure. Doing so offers grace and a path to restoration to the worker, first. Taking this step first keeps all the kingdom principles of scripture alive in the Organization within the discipline plan. If workers are tied intimately to The Boss and have been managed carefully, including previous discussions about the area in which they are failing, the bond of unity and peace between all members of the Organization can and will be maintained.

For Step One to be successful, these principles need to be clear.

- The worker understands they have entered the discipline plan.
- The overseer is clear about the nature of the failure.
- The overseer interviews the worker to secure an understanding of the cause of the failure and the two agree about the cause.
- The overseer assumes responsibility for the failure.
- The overseer eliminates the root of the cause. (i.e., with training, resetting expectations, providing resources, restoring relationships, deliverance from distractions or overburdening, etc.)
- Both the worker and the overseer document the meeting and agree to terms for improvement, which have been provided by the overseer and both sign the document.

After step one is taken, the worker returns to work on their assigned responsibility understanding exactly how to succeed.

Step Two

If the same worker persists with the same failure, the burden of responsibility shifts from the overseer to the worker. This step engages the worker both in the seriousness of the failure and their need to assume personal responsibility for success.

For Step Two to be successful, these points need to be clear.

- The overseer reiterates the nature of the failure and the root cause and gets agreement with the worker about both.
- The overseer explains that the worker is entering the second phase of the discipline plan.
- The overseer offers the worker a performance agreement, which is a formal document outlining these points.

  » The specific failure
  » The specific behavior to remedy the failure
  » The measurement(s) that will be used to determine if the failure is corrected
  » The time frame over which the performance agreement will remain in place

» The understanding that the worker will enter the third phase of discipline if the failure persists during the terms of the performance agreement

- Both the worker and the overseer sign the document.

With the performance agreement in place, the worker returns to his/her responsibilities understanding the terms of success.

Step Three

If the failures persist during the performance agreement as determined by the established measurements, the worker is relieved of their responsibilities. If the worker is an employee, that means termination.

If the worker is determined to be of such value to the Organization in other ways or capacities, there remains an option to reassign them to a different set of responsibilities.

Sometimes it's through failure in one area that a significant competency is discovered in another area. Many Organizations refer to this as getting the round pegs in the round holes.

Summary of People Management
and Discipline for the Church

- Train everyone so that they know exactly how they will be managed during the normal course of work.
- Train everyone so that they know exactly how they will be handled if they fail.
- Follow through on the principles that have been taught.
- Treat everyone in the Organization exactly the same!

CHAPTER 8
Master Planning

If there is one event in the life of a congregation to highlight each year, it would be the Master Planning process. It's the all in, everyone involved, totally focused event to which everyone in the Organization should look forward each year. There are several reasons for this being the case.

- When seeking the direction of The Boss, everyone should be given an opportunity to be involved. Because the people occupy the second layer of the Org Chart, they should be comprehensively informed of, aware of, and invested in the Master Planning process.
- The congregation should understand that the Master Plan will drive everything that will get done during the upcoming year. Ministry Leaders who will answer the seven questions that form the plan will be committed to following their plans for the

next year; therefore, the congregation's prayers for them during this process are critical to its success.

When the plan is finalized, there will be significant congregational buy in for it by since they have been involved in the process of formulating it. The ideas in the plan will not have to be "sold" to them. They will look forward to reading the plan and continuing to pray for its success when it has been completed.

If there is any event significant enough to promote and publicize with banners and balloons every year, it's the Master Planning process. Everyone should know about it, involve themselves in it, and celebrate it!

It must be clear to all Ministry Leaders who will be drawing up the plan, that the Master Plan will be the control document for managing the cumulative efforts of the congregation to speak love to God for the next year. During this process, the most fervent prayers for God's direction for each ministry must be prayed. Also, during this process, Ministry Leaders will be evaluating their willingness and passion to continue leading ministries for another year.

If a Ministry Leader is not led by the Spirit to continue a particular ministry for another year, the Executive Team will be talking to The Boss about whether that given ministry is sufficiently mission critical that someone should be sought and found to continue it, to let it lie dormant for a year, or to allow it to go out of existence. Every ministry of the church should have a gifted leader leading it. Every Ministry Leader, with the help of The Boss, must lay out a plan for their ministry every year.

Ministry Leaders should never fear this process. It is the time for honesty and openness about effectiveness and success on the part of every leader. This is the time for personal soul-searching and faith in The Boss who is whispering, "Trust Me," into their ears. Ministry Leaders should feel unified by the process, knowing that every one of their brothers and sisters who are leading ministries are walking the same path with them, just like Jehoshaphat experienced in 2 Chronicles 20!

The Seven Questions

These are seven questions every Ministry Leader must answer for the Organization to complete their contribution to the Master Plan.

1. How does this ministry contribute to speaking love to The Boss? Does it focus on one language more than the others? If so, which ones? Why? (Adoration, Transformation, Companionship, Compassion, Partnership, Evangelism)

    Every person who functions as a part of every ministry of the church MUST feel a connection to one or more of the Love Languages being spoken to God and Ministry Leaders must understand how their ministries connect to that goal. The answer to this question demonstrates the Ministry Leader's understanding of that connection.

2. Is there is a specific segment of the Organization on which this ministry focuses? If so, please identify it and explain why. (i.e., senior saints, musicians, children, youth, men, women, couples, singles, building and grounds, etc.)

   The answer to this question helps identify whether the ministry is Love Language based or demographically based. Neither is preferred over the other. This answer refines the focus of the ministry. It helps volunteers better understand the focus and nature of the ministry and helps the Executive Team evaluate how It contributes to the overall health of the Organization.

3. Briefly outline the functionality of this ministry. What does it accomplish? (i.e., It feeds and clothes needy people. It prepares and leads weekly worship. It's a Bible Study. It aids in the process of divorce recovery., etc.) Provide sufficient detail that a new member of the Organization would get a good enough idea of how the ministry functions to know whether or not they may want to volunteer to be a part of it.

   This answer explains the function of the ministry. Although this outline should be brief, a paragraph or two, it should give any reader a simple, yet sufficient, understanding of what might be expected of them if they volunteered to be a part of it. This answer also contributes to deeper understanding of the ministry for the Executive Team.

4. How will success be measured in this ministry? What

are the expected outcomes from it? In what ways will it please The Boss?

This answer sets the goals for the ministry. If those are objective goals they can be expressed with numbers and totals. If they are less tangible, they should still be described in subjective terms. This answer lets everyone know what drives the Ministry Leader in this effort. It also allows the Executive Team to know if the Ministry Leader is being realistic or if their reach is exceeding their grasp.

5. What are the building use requirements of this ministry? Did this ministry have a budget last year? What is the proposed budget this year for this ministry?

At some point, an evaluation of resources must be made about each ministry effort of the church. This is typically known as a cost/benefit analysis or return on investment estimate.

The answer to this question helps the financial people know how much should be allocated to each ministry when the budget is developed. Ministry Leaders need to be completely open and honest about their real needs in answer to this question.

6. Is this a new ministry? If this ministry was included in last year's Master Plan, are there significant changes proposed for this year? New goals? Expansion or contraction?

The answer to this question lets the Organization know about new ministries as they occur. This gives the church an opportunity to celebrate successes which require expanded efforts in any given ministry area. It also allows the Executive Team to know when a Ministry Leader may be less passionate or even disengaged from a ministry. In such cases, their response must be addressed according to the people management principles outlined previously.

7. Briefly outline the training plan for incorporating new volunteers into this ministry.

Every ministry of the church must be prepared to assimilate new people into their efforts. No one knows when The Boss may send a new talent into the Organization that can bring new life, new ideas, and new value to a ministry. Ministry Leaders must have a plan ready for incorporating new people including process outlines, role descriptions, clear expectations, and FAQ sheets.

Accessibility of the Master Plan

The Master Plan drives everything the church attempts to accomplish; therefore, it is essential that the plan be available to everyone in the Organization. Whether online or in booklet form, everyone should be able to easily access its content in order to know what's going on! Smaller churches will have fewer Ministries and therefore a smaller Master Plan. Larger churches will have more pages in their plan. The concern is not how much is done compared to any other church. The concern is whether God is accomplishing what He wants to do in every church, whether large or small. After it is compiled, the Master Plan has a variety of uses.

- It is used by new members to know how and where to invest their talents in the ministry efforts of the church.
- It is used by those working with the finances in order to develop annual budgets. (See Chapter 10, Page 109.)
- It is used by the Executive Team to evaluate the health of the Organization and to know how to approach The Boss about any deficiencies they may find in the church's ability to speak the Six Love Languages.
- It is used by the church at large for encouragement of Ministry Leaders and the focusing of their prayers for the Organization.
- It is used by Ministry Leaders, Staff Leaders, and the Executive Team who watch for the overlapping, duplication, and collaboration of efforts. This same group uses it to develop calendars for building use, special events and ministry projection into the communities they serve.

Mileposts in the Master Planning Process

- **The Kickoff**

  Names and faces of every Ministry Leader who will be contributing to the plan are posted for the Organization. Include both full-time and part time paid staff, as well as lay leaders, making no distinction between them. Use every outlet available to place the names and faces of Ministry Leaders before the congregation.

- **Looking to the Boss for Guidance**

  Plan a day of fasting and a season of prayer to cover the weeks of planning. Fasting does not have to be food but could apply to social media or other distractions. Have everyone fast on the same day for 24 hours beginning at six o'clock one evening and ending at six o'clock the next. If the planning process takes a month to complete, then keep these leaders on the hearts of the people with promotion and announcements all month long.

- **Compilation**

  Have a compilation team in place that organizes, formats, and arranges the plans into a booklet as they are submitted. Don't wait until all the plans are turned in to begin and continue this process. Particularly in the first year, do not be disappointed if reminders and follow-up are necessary to complete the plan. Push for it, but if you do not get 100% participation in the first year, publish the plan anyway.

- **Celebration**

  After it is complete, celebrate the plan and make it accessible to everyone in the Organization. Use it for all the purposes discussed earlier. Keep it in front of the people constantly.

In summary, the Master Planning process should be an all-inclusive effort by the entire church. It should be as momentous an event as exists on the church's calendar. The process of praying for it, writing it, compiling it, and celebrating it should draw the congregation together in unity and enthusiasm. When it is published and distributed, it should represent the direction of The Boss for the coming year.

CHAPTER 9
Key Measurables

Every corporation knows the value of measuring as it proportionately relates to success. You cannot evaluate what you cannot measure. You cannot improve what you cannot measure. Whatever you measure will be the focus of attention for whomever is producing the product. Measuring finds problems and bottlenecks in processes. Measuring determines benchmarks for continuous improvement. Measuring finds the parameters of variation in any process. If you want to get better at nearly anything, you must find something to measure.

The key to measuring is knowing what to measure and when to measure it. Before the quality revolution hit America most American companies measured their products after they were finished. In other words, they discovered whether a product was worth selling after it was complete. The Japanese were way ahead of the Americans at the time and were already measuring the production processes as products were being made. When a product moved from one part of an assembly line to another, the Japanese already knew whether they were moving a good part or a bad part to the next stage of manufacturing. They understood the concept of competing on the basis of quality, not merely cost and convenience.

Two more points need to be made before ending this example.

- Nearly all companies these days have figured out their measurements and have adapted their software well enough so that they can statistically figure out how they are doing in near real time! Concepts like "Just In Time" inventory measurements and days of sales costs, as well as the ratios between costs like overhead, marketing, direct labor, and indirect labor can be and are calculated on the fly. These don't include the ratios between gross margin, net margin, and net profit. Understand that corporations do not market themselves based on these statistics, but they certainly determine their health by them.

- The CFO is not the CEO for a reason. CFOs are so driven by numbers indicating health and profit that they can easily drive a company away from one product line into another. A company can be making soap one week and ice cream the next if a CFO is allowed to alter the mission of a company in response to what they see as a better, more profitable market with less investment (a better ROI). The CEO is there to keep the company's purpose, mission, and direction in line with its founding.

So it is with the church. We cannot alter the function of the church just because we are better at creating and sustaining social clubs than we are at making disciples. Neither can we begin to measure only the things we are good at so we can keep feeling good about ourselves when quite possibly we are realistically unhealthy.

There are two questions for the church to ask when determining the health of their Organization.

- What should we be measuring?
- When should we measure it?

The most obvious answers to these two questions are not necessarily the correct ones. Most churches, whether large or small, might quickly answer, "Attendances and offerings!" Measuring success in the church by attendance and giving statistics is like what American companies were doing while the Japanese were way ahead of them in measuring products after they had left the assembly line, instead of measuring the production processes.

Attendance and offering totals can be measured in the church and positive growth in either one or both is a helpful indicator, but they can be artificially produced without the true purpose of the church being achieved. Using them as the indicators of the real health of the Organization can be very misleading and has driven many churches away from their foundational principles in order produce positive results in both categories. It's possible for a church to maintain a significant and an impressive annual budget with very few disciples!

If the process of producing disciples is measured, and the success of an Organization is determined by the proportion of people attending who are effectively loving God back, then numeric growth in attendance and giving has real meaning, as long as equally proportionate numbers of disciples continue to grow with the attendance and giving. Since they represent results more than targets, I will leave attendance and giving statistics out of the discussion of key measurables.

By now you may think that I have abused your time by repeatedly bringing up the Six Love Languages for your consideration; however, as much as I have mentioned their critical relationship to success in the church, I have not discussed how or when to measure them. They are the Key Measurables when determining the health of any church, no matter the size of its average attendance or budget!

Let's review them and determine how to measure them.

Adoration

If you were to measure the "adoration factor" in your marriage, what would you look for? Probably the three words of authenticity, expression, and passion would be used in the description of your giving or receiving of adoration. Telling God how much you love Him with the Language of Adoration is very much the same.

Authenticity is about genuineness, believability, and credibility. Jesus said to the woman at the well in John 4 that His disciples must worship Him in spirit and truth. He said this to declare a new standard for worship apart from keeping the laws about it. True worship needs to be authentic worship in His Kingdom.

Expression is the action part of praise. It's all about what you do and say to release your convictions. For your wife or husband, to express adoration you might buy something, go somewhere, write something, or even sing something! As I've already written, praise is never passive in scripture and never reduced to a thought, but rather, it's always overtly expressed.

Passion is all about how you feel about what you are expressing. If someone means a great deal to you, your expression of love for them would never lack intensity or dynamics. In fact, if they were the most important person on earth to you, probably you would be unable to control the passion you would express for them.

Methods of Measurement:
- During corporate worship, place (or hide) a video camera in the front of your sanctuary facing the congregation to capture images of them while participating in corporate worship. Ask a discrete, select group of people to evaluate it afterward for the three characteristics of authenticity, expression, and passion just described.
- Offer your people an anonymous survey to tell you about the praise that is ongoing in their personal lives apart from corporate worship. Ask questions such as, "How often are you prompted to praise God during the week? How do you release your praise when you are in private? How emotional do you get when praising God by yourself? What time of day is your favorite for individual praise to God?"
- On a Likert scale of 1-10, conduct an anonymous survey of your people for the difference in their adoration for

God upon entering your Sunday worship service versus when they leave.

Transformation: *Part I*

Two factors are true about faith.

- If faith doesn't produce action, it doesn't exist.
- If a person does not add to faith other virtues, they'll lose sight of it. (James 2 and 2 Peter 1)

We treat faith as if its only connection to our lives is its role in our salvation and its ability to get our prayers answered. We treat the rest of our lives as if God will manipulate every circumstance to our advantage and we'll end up healthy, wealthy and wise, but the Bible seems to indicate that our faith should also be transformative.

Our lives are to be demonstrations of how faith results in growth and fruit-bearing. It is true that faith plays its role in regenerating us in an instant with spiritual re- birth as old things pass away and everything becomes new. However, that new, infantile person we've become has a lifetime of transformation, growth, and obedience ahead. It is in our willingness to allow the Holy Spirit to control us that God hears in another language how much we love Him back.

As we give the Holy Spirit control, we begin to speak and act more and more like Jesus. We learn to laugh at the things He thinks are funny and cry over the things that make Him sad. We learn to value the people He values and speak the truth in love as He did. We make choices in moments of temptation like He made them. We pull our children close and forgive others as He forgave us. Our humility and compassion flow from us in the same way it flows from Him. In every outward act that demonstrates the transformation of our inner person, God hears us whispering our love for Him.

The church is in the business of teaching people how to let the Holy Spirit have control of their lives. It teaches its members how to live by, be led by, and to keep in step with Him. It teaches these lessons by the examples of its leaders and the teachings of its Ministry Leaders and Staff Leaders. It is, therefore, a love language to be measured for results in terms of the spiritual growth of the members of the Organization.

Method of Measurement:
- In small groups, such as Life Groups or Sunday School Classes, have your people rate their ability to produce each of the nine fruits of the Spirit on a daily basis using a Likert scale from 1-10, 1 being almost never and 10 being almost always. Have them do this anonymously and turn in their results. The nine fruits of the Spirit are love, joy, peace, patience, kindness, goodness, faithfulness, gentleness, and self-control. Repeat this process periodically, perhaps twice annually, with these same groups watching for trends.

Transformation: *Part II*

Transformation is always dependent on the teachings of scripture, so it is imperative that the congregation be constantly immersed in the teachings of the Word of God. There is no way to understand the mind of Christ without studying, even memorizing, the words of Christ. There are three levels of learning required.

- **The Bible should be read.**

  We often use the Bible more as a textbook than as a glimpse into the mind of God. Reading the story of the relationship between man and God from the beginning and as it developed is a valuable exercise. People should be encouraged to read large quantities of scripture in single sittings. Read an entire gospel, a whole letter or epistle, several chapters of Old Testament history without stressing over what is not completely understood. Read the Bible like you would read a novel getting to know the characters and identifying with them. In this way, the reader begins to rub shoulders with prophets, kings, followers, Pharisees, disciples, sinners, and Jesus. Reading God's Word changes lives!

- **The Bible should be studied.**

  Much of what the Bible means cannot be easily interpreted by simply reading it. When factors, such as writers, speakers, audiences, timing, occasions, problems, and perceptions are considered, they can alter the meaning of a passage, sometimes even entire books for the reader. When appropriate understanding is given to the context of a passage, there are other factors to be considered in the course of study (i.e., the book theme, the longer view of the context of the verses being studied, the numbers of paragraphs in which the author stays on a particular subject, the sentence structures being used, the argumentation being sustained, and the authors own statements of purpose). A disciple must be dedicated to study, study, study, in order to rightly handle the Word of God!

- **The Bible should be memorized.**
There is a direct connection between the work of the Holy Spirit in a person's heart and the biblical knowledge in the mind of every person. While giving some His final words to His followers in John 14, Jesus told them that the promised Holy Spirit would remind them of the things He had taught them. That promised functionality of the Holy Spirit is unchanged. We must frustrate the Holy Spirit because He would rush to remind us of the words of Jesus if we just knew a few more of them. Hiding His words in our hearts gives the Holy Spirit something with which to work and there is no other means besides memorization.

Methods of Measurement:
- Numbers of Chapters read by a specific group of the congregation or the entire congregation
- Numbers of people involved in John's Accountability Model during which scriptures are memorized by two people
- Numbers of Bible studies that study strictly from the text of the Bible
- Numbers of apt teachers of the Bible available to the congregation

Companionship

The standard of health we are using for the church comes from Acts 2:42-47 and Acts 4:32-35. In the verses in Acts 2 the word "together" appears three times. Most of the activity found in all these verses highlights the togetherness the early church enjoyed. They spent a lot of time together, did a lot of things together, supported each other with abandon, and while doing so they enjoyed the favor of all the people around them. WOW! I don't know how you react to such a revelation, but I am more than impressed by this group of young Christians. They obviously knew how to speak the Love Language of Companionship extremely well! They were just flat fun to be around!

The detailed descriptions of what are held as appropriate interpersonal interactions in the church are found in the "One Anothers" of scripture. The culture every church leader would love to see among the members of the Organization is detailed by them. Measuring their existence and acceptance, then using them as the established protocol for behavior in the church, is critical.

Methods of Measurement:
- Leader observation is a subjective measurement. Most Ministry Leaders, Staff Leaders, and Executive Team members will be of sufficient spiritual maturity to measure how well the Organization has incorporated the "One Anothers" into the culture of the church. Ask these leaders to rate what they have seen and heard over a given period of time, giving them a specific list from which to work. Repeat this periodically.

- In Life Groups or Sunday School Classes, periodically give members lists of about of the "One Anothers," and ask them to rate their importance to the effectiveness of the church. Keep doing this over the course of several months and watch for trends.
- Survey Life Groups or Sunday School Classes referencing a list of the "One Anothers," which ones are most frequently implemented in the normal course of the lives of their group, with each other, and within the communities in which they live. Rate them from most to least used.

Compassion

Few of all the love languages we can speak to God speak louder than the Language of Compassion. How the people of the church treat hurting people tells God volumes about what is in their hearts. When God gathers His people together at the return of Jesus, He will separate them based on their responses to and treatment of hurting people. (Matthew 25) Whether or not we measure compassion now, God will certainly measure this love language when He brings history to an end.

There are two categories of measurements that can help leadership understand the health of the Organization regarding its benevolent heart.

Methods of Measurement:
- In dollars, time, and numbers of individuals and families assisted, statistics can (and should) be gathered by Ministry Leaders who administrate programming to help hurting people. These statistics should be published and

given to the people of the church for their continuing interest in these kinds of ministry efforts and for their prayers.

- If special events are conducted by church programming, statistics about these events should be gathered similarly to ongoing programming numbers and published for the church (i.e., benevolence dollars donated during a campaign, gifts and/or food given away at Christmas, school children assisted with food, clothing or supplies each year, etc.).

- Anonymous surveys of the entire congregation can be conducted to simply capture a glimpse of the kinds of personal, benevolent assistance being given to hurting people in the communities the church serves. Statistics in the same three categories will help the church understand the impact it is making with the language of compassion.

Partnership

When one side of a relationship does all the giving and the other does all the receiving, the relationship never feels like it is functioning the way it should. Whether in friendships, marriages, or even at work, the same principle applies. The church should feel the same way about its relationship to The Boss. There are definitely some things we can only receive from Him because we have no power to produce them for ourselves; however, our Boss wants to partner with us in His kingdom work and scripture makes that abundantly clear. There are two areas where partnering with God are clearly identifiable.

- **The investments of our giftedness**

  When The Boss gifts us with functional gifs to contribute to His Organization, He does not expect us to keep them for ourselves. He has high expectations for the return He may get by their being invested in His work as is illustrated in Matthew 25, the parable of the talents. By using the list of gifts found in Romans 12, we can create a list of ministry efforts the people of the church should be making as functional parts of it. When they use their gifts, they are partnering with God in His venture on earth and should recognize that they are speaking love to Him by doing so.

- **The money given or spent on behalf of the ministry of the church**

  The Boss makes it clear that you can look at the monetary investments a person makes and see what is most important in their hearts. To partner with Him means to invest dollars in that partnership. (See Chapter 13, Page 155.) When God sees us treasuring people and using money, rather than treasuring money and using people, He hears us speaking love to Him!

Methods of Measurement:
- Survey the Ministry Leaders of your church who are listed in the Master Plan and calculate the total number of people involved in the ministries of the church. Create a ratio between the average attendance in worship on Sunday mornings and the number of members involved

in ministries to determine the Organization's real functionality.

- Anonymously survey your congregation to determine the percentage of dollars given verses the dollars earned to establish the giving capacity of the membership with reference to the tithe.
- Set aside one Sunday each year for all members to bring the tithe into the storehouse of the church. No matter whether any given member tithes on any other Sunday, on the designated Sunday ask everyone to bring an offering that represents their tithe, based on their weekly income. This offering will help to establish the giving capacity of the church.

Evangelism

There is an urgency in the mission of the church that is satisfied more by the Language of Evangelism than any other. It is getting the call of the gospel, the good news, into the lives of people who have either never heard it or never responded to it. The urgency comes from the brevity of every life on earth and the singular opportunity every person gets to respond to God's love for them in Jesus. A language that is typically learned and spoken by a few special people in each church is a language that needs to be taught to and spoken by everyone in the Organization. There are many methods of both learning and speaking this language in various books and online sources. (See Chapter 12, Page 127.)

If you really wanted to tell me how much you loved me, and you knew me well, you'd know what you really needed to do was brag on my kids and grandkids. Nothing about me amounts to as much as what I feel for my kids. Speaking love to me is all about asking about, talking about, and bragging about my kids.

Can you imagine how much more God feels about the accomplishments of HIS SON, Jesus? How clearly do you think He hears us speak our love for Him when we brag about His Son to other people?

Methods of Measurement:
- Ask every visitor who registers their attendance in your worship service to explain how they were introduced to the congregation (i.e., social media, personal invitation, attended a special event first, etc.).
- Measure the trend in conversion experiences year to year.
- Survey your Life Group members or Sunday School Class attenders regarding the numbers of people to whom they have introduced Jesus, in a week, a month, a year, or ever!
- Measure the numbers of people trained by church programming to present the gospel to others every year.

CAUTION!!!
There are two rules to follow when surveying any group in the church about anything.

- Never survey a group without returning the results of the survey back to the group when it is concluded. If statistics are developed, return the high, low, and average in every case.

- Never survey a group about a subject matter about which you are unprepared to make changes with respect to their responses. One of the most detrimental things that can happen to morale is to ask a person's opinion about something, then make no response after they give it to you. Feedback and change must happen after every survey you conduct. Don't survey your people until you are prepared to provide feedback and make changes!

Surveys are inherently subjective. They are not the best at creating accurate data points to plot and review. Since what is being measured are Love Languages, there are few better tools to use that are an improvement on them. People must be shown that measurements are a first step toward a more effective and successful future, and that we are taking these measurements as One Body.

Remember that people will tend to focus on anything you measure! So, make sure you're ready to respond to their feedback before you ask for it.

CHAPTER 10
Budgeting, Finance, and Properties

The Galilean women who were helping finance Jesus' ministry must have not known that Judas occasionally helped himself to some of Jesus's ministry money. Had they known, there most certainly would have been a ruckus! (Mark 15:41; John 12:6) Transparency about finances with the Organization is imperative! All too often, churches have come to believe that a select group of people should be the only ones totally aware of how much money is coming in, how much is going out, and how it is being spent. That kind of church financial management theory is anathema!

By placing all the people of the church in the second layer of the Organizational chart, they have been positioned to remain constantly informed about the financial position of the Organization. No corporation would keep such a layer uninformed about its finances. A critically important lesson to learn about church finances is to keep everyone fully informed!

Plan-Based Budgeting

As many times as it has been used as a tool to increase faith, planning a budget is not the time to test a congregation's commitment to giving. Budgeting is when the Organization should see faithful stewardship given to their offerings by seeing them carefully allocated to the needs of the Master Plan. If putting together the Master Plan is an all-inclusive event in which the entire Organization participates by seeking direction from The Boss, then following up with a budget driven by its requirements will make perfect sense to the Organization. That is exactly how the congregation should see the budgeting process work.

When every Ministry Leader completes their contribution to the plan by answering the seven questions, a skeletal budget should already be established. The Executive Team needs only to review the Master Plan for its ability to keep the Organization healthy and in balance regarding its ability to effectively speak all Six Love Languages.

The Executive Team should also make certain the Organization is capable of funding the plan with average giving as forecast from previous giving years (units) and current trends. There may be a need to request changes in funding requests from Ministry Leaders after the Master Plan is examined for its requirements. These conversations must be kept open and fair to all Ministry Leaders.

After the general budget is established, targets for expansion and contraction should also be established. It is appropriate to tell the Organization how its funds will be spent if God blesses the Organization, and actual giving exceeds the needs of the budget. Targets for 5%, 10%, or even 15% are appropriate. It is with these targets that the congregation can be challenged for increased giving.

At the same time, the Organization should understand how cuts will be made if giving falls short of budget requirements and targets of 5%, 10%, or even 15% are appropriate. By giving the Organization the understanding that its Executive Team is preparing for any eventuality, confidence and trust are built, year by year.

No other area of breached trust will destroy the enthusiasm and drive of a congregation more quickly than spending funds on non-budgeted items without disclosure. Doing so is like a shepherd protecting a wolf instead of the flock.

Budget approval is handled differently in various congregations. Four basic principles help to keep the structure of the Org Chart effectively and functionally in place.

Principle One

Prior to approval, inform the congregation. The proposed budget should accompany the Master Plan and copies of it should be given to the entire Organization.

Principle Two

Use a group larger than the Executive Team to approve the budget. This could include Staff Leaders, Ministry Leaders, and possibly even the entire Organization.

Principle Three

Avoid voting! Use consensus-building techniques to gain acceptance and consent for the budget. Seek support rather than up or down approval.

Principle Four

Once approved, maintain easy access to the budget for the Organization.

Plan-Based Accounting

Following approval, the Master Plan and budget drive the efforts of the Organization each year. Every ministry listed in the plan should be assigned an individual number, as well as sub-numbers, to account for the spending that occurs within that ministry. Ministry Leaders should have real time access to their accounts. The sub-numbers should be assigned by the Ministry Leaders in ways that effectively describe the areas of effort they will be giving their ministries. The control of spending should be left in the hands of the Ministry Leaders who must be allowed to make spending decisions for their areas of the Organization. They must be cautioned to keep their efforts and spending within the limits set by The Master Plan and the budget. Changes to those limits represent changes that need exposure to and support of the Organization.

Extenuating circumstances will require changes to both the Master Plan and budget. When our church was working through the COVID-19 Pandemic, we were kept from our normal routine. New plans were implemented, and the budget was flexed to meet the new demands. All layers of the Org Chart must keep their eyes on fulfilling the demands of the Six Love Languages, as well as meeting the needs of the communities they serve, while willingly adapting when necessary. Five basic principles will help the Organization understand its financial position.

Principle One

Allow everyone to see the tie between a ministry's plan and its spending. Prayer support, encouragement of leaders, and financial support will follow as the Organization sees repeated success in any given ministry.

Principle Two

Keep everyone accountable to the Master Plan and the budget. It will strengthen the annual planning process, as well as the funding necessary to accomplish the plan.

Principle Three

Keeping the accounting ledgers simple, clear, and accessible will answer many questions before they are asked.

Principle Four

An annual audit by an independent entity will protect the treasurer, the leadership team, and the Organization.

Principle Five

A summary of actual giving versus budget requirements is helpful. With online giving and other means of making donations, a monthly summary can be kept most accurately.

Communicating with the Organization

Financial discussions may seem difficult, but that does not make them avoidable. One of the top three causes of marital difficulties arises when couples or families are unable to approach the subject of income versus spending. This applies to the church, as well. The answer is to make steady progress toward total disclosure with the Organization. The more they know, the more they will stay engaged. The more they will see the effects of their giving, the more joy they will embrace in the church's successes.

Caution One

Constant communication does not mean constant appeals. Communication about the financial health of the Organization must not be continuously tied to appeals for more funds. It is defeating for a congregation to believe that they are honoring God with their giving, but the sum of what they give is never enough to meet the ministry needs of their Organization. The Master Planning and budgeting processes must be openly transparent to them and must result in an effective and achievable plan and budget. Members of the Organization will recognize that what has been planned will need their financial support. The Executive Team should not place the Organization under continuous financial stress resulting in constant appeals for ever greater offering totals.

Caution Two

Campaigning for funds carries with it some negative consequences. There exist many parachurch financial consultants who guarantee increased giving if hired. Their methods should be held in suspicion for two reasons.

- Consultants tend to teach a 'give to get' theology that is more destructive to an individual's faith than instructive to a disciple's walk with God.
- When consultants complete their work, many individuals are left to recreate their personal family budgets which changes the joy of giving to the Organization into what feels to them like paying more bills. Neither of these consequences is helpful to either the long-term growth of disciples or the financial health of the Organization.

If the church trusts The Boss to lead every member into an intimate walk with Him, biblical teaching on giving will give the Organization the funds HE requires to complete HIS work. Keep the congregation informed, be good stewards, trust The Boss, understand that possessions possess.

It seems to me that our goal verses from Acts 2:42-47 and Acts 4:32-35 speak much more about church members selling properties and giving away the proceeds than they do about the church as an Organization owning properties.

It is not an irreconcilable conundrum that the Organization might own properties or buildings, but with this cautionary thought. Every possession owned comes not only with its original cost, but also the costs of retaining it.

Possessions tend to possess their possessors. The church ought always to be carefully strategic when thinking of owning anything, especially properties and buildings.

Quite possibly, some old traditions were brought from Europe when our founders came to the shores of the New World and established churches here in America. Perhaps they longed to see the colonies dotted with the same elaborate cathedrals they had left behind. Perhaps the concept of honor for God included buildings whose architecture would bring them to the awe they wanted to feel when meeting with others for worship. Maybe they longed to see the sunlight filtering through stained glass windows because of how it made them feel when they worshiped, prayed, or communed with the Master. These traditions have been handed down through centuries of history.

It may be possible that the contemporary church believes it needs buildings and properties to make statements of success to the communities they serve. Perhaps current thinking makes us believe there is a need for a point of reference, a place, a look, a familiarity to which the people can rally on Sundays.

No matter what has precipitated our interest, there is a point to be pondered every time a church considers buying properties or building buildings.

Evangelism to be asked and answered is how will this help us speak more clearly the Six Love Languages God longs to hear from us? Property will cost not only what is spent on it now, but later in costs of maintenance, renovation, remodeling, repair, and eventually even replacement. All of this is an effort to honor God who describes our lives here like living in tents while we await our home with Him, in a building not built by human hands, an eternal house in heaven whose architect and builder is God, Himself (II Corinthians 5). We should give significant strategic consideration to anything purchased or built in the name of honoring Him.

CHAPTER 11
Vision and Methods

The purpose of the church,
Helping People Love God Back, never changes.

The mission of the church,
Making Disciples, never changes.

The vision and methods of the church
flex based on varying factors.

Vision can be equated with a philosophic approach. A church's vision answers questions of who, what, how, when, and where to best encourage a group of people in a particular locale to speak the Six Love Languages to God. Answers to those questions will vary based on factors such as: ethnic diversity, median age, location, local culture, history, growth potential, and certain theologies and traditions. Having identified the measurements of a healthy church, there remains a task for each church to determine how to achieve maximum health given their local factors.

Unfortunately, most recently there has been a trend for churches to copy whatever the growing churches in their area are doing as measured by attendance and giving totals. This trend has led many churches into wasteful, exhausting, and expensive efforts that have yielded minimal results. Every church must seek the leading of The Boss when arriving at their particular vision. What has been lacking has been an effective process to determine that vision.

Methods follow after vision is established. Methods can be equated with programs and plans as they are the means of accomplishing the vision. Methods fall under the scriptural description of becoming all things to all people in order to save some. Methods are created by the people God gifts in the Organization to help everyone speak one or more of the Six Love Languages to God.

Methods flex and change based on the gifting of the Ministry Leader implementing them. For a church to attain and maintain health, an atmosphere of flexibility regarding methods must be developed and incorporated into the culture.

This posture presents its own set of difficulties for some congregations that have reached a status quo in their choice of methods, which have been accepted as the way things should be done. There has been very little offered to the church by way of process to break through these barriers allowing for the leadership of The Boss to drive the Organization toward new methods.

The key in both cases is that all the members of any given church must sense that what they are attempting to do is exactly what God wants them to do. If there are differing opinions or a lack of consensus in this regard, the church will be dysfunctional and lack the drive and enthusiasm it will take to achieve success. An effective process that involves the whole Organization can and will bring a given group together around its vision and chosen methods.

Jehoshaphat does many good things as a leader of the people of Judah when faced with an insurmountable enemy and no vision for the future as evidenced by the final words of his prayer, "We do not know what to do, but our eyes are on you." (II Chronicles 20)

The Vision
Process

Step One:
Use the measurements!

The vision for the future of any church must result from its pursuit of overall health. The process of developing a vision starts with the Executive Team's analysis of data derived from the measurements taken from each of the Six Love Languages. (See Chapter 9, Page 97.) This analysis includes input from Staff Leaders and Ministry Leaders requiring brainstorming sessions with the combined groups. From this input, the Executive Team begins to build a picture of the Organization's strengths and weaknesses. Before any conclusions are drawn about the picture that is being developed, move to Step Two!

Step Two:
Talk to The Boss!

It is amazing how many Executive Teams or vision planning teams sit in church classrooms and basements late into the night to debate the future of their Organizations without truly seeking the leadership and direction of The Boss! The second step in discovering a clear vision for any church is talking to The Boss.

This step should include fasting, praying, waiting, listening, and leaning into the Holy Spirit. As the team coalesces around its consensus regarding their understanding of what God wants from the church, they must formulate a statement in order to enlarge their prayer circle to include the prayers of the entire congregation.

Congregational prayers may include these thoughts.

- We believe God is challenging us to look at the way we speak the Language of Adoration to Him.
- We believe God is asking us to look at our disciple-making process, pressing us all toward higher levels of spiritual transformation.
- We believe God wants us to build deeper levels of connectivity in the relationships in the church.
- We believe God is opening our eyes to help more hurting people in our community
- We believe God is pushing us toward greater partnerships with Him as it regards the investments we are each making in His kingdom.

- We believe God is calling us to greater levels of commitment regarding the telling of the story of Jesus to our community.

This statement is followed by a challenge for the congregation to fast and pray with the Executive Team, Staff Leaders, and Ministry Leaders as the entire Organization seeks the will of The Boss. This step in the process should include ideas similar to these.

- A time frame for the season of prayer
- Sufficient promotion to keep the season of prayer in the minds and hearts of the people for the entire time frame
- A prayer vigil should be organized. It could be a special service for just one evening; or up to a 24-hour vigil with a very directed focus.
- The season of prayer should include everyone, even the children as Jehoshaphat did!

This season of prayer should end with consensus among the members of the Executive Team regarding the vision God wants the church to pursue. If there is no consensus, do not proceed and report back to the Organization.

Step Three:
Announce the vision statement
to the congregation.

Step Four:
Hand the vision statement to consultants
for refinement, clarification,
and possible solutions.

It is possible that one or two Executive Team members would assist the consultants, but the Staff Leaders and/or Ministry Leaders who comprise the consultant team should not be incumbered by making this group too large. The consultants use the Problem-Solving process to hone, clarify, and create possible solutions for improvement. As the consultant team does its work, there may be a need for more data collection or input from various segments of the Organization. This team should have the freedom to include anyone they deem necessary as they do their work.

The results of this team's work should include changes in methods or programs necessary to execute the new vision. It is not, however, a detailed plan at this point, only a clear vision. Executable plans are developed later in the process.

Step Five:
The Consultants report their findings
to the Executive Team.

The Consultants report their findings to the Executive Team and more honing takes place. This may require a series of meetings but should not exceed two or three. A final version of the vision is established.

Step Six:
The fully developed vision is presented
to the Organization.

The fully developed vision is presented to the Organization as the consensus opinion of all those involved in its development. A congregational meeting may possibly be necessary, depending on the size and scope of the changes being proposed; however, any presentation should be accompanied by printed copies and online access to the information presented. A format for answers to the congregation's questions and input should be established. There should be no Q and A or back and forth at the congregational meeting, but there should be ample time given for it after the vision has been presented to the Organization.

Step Seven:
The consultant team begins to turn
the vision into plans.

While a period of Q and A and input from the congregation proceeds, the consultant team begins to turn the vision into plans. This conversion details the specific methods, program changes, training, physical renovations, etc. necessary to implement the plans. Measurements are developed that will give critical feedback to the Ministry Leaders responsible for the implementation as the plan is launched. A launch date is projected, and the plan becomes complete.

Step Eight:
Introduce the plan to the congregation.

Another meeting of the entire Organization is called and the plan explained. Access to the plan should be made available in print, as well as online. The launch date is established, and the congregation continues to pray for success!

Step Nine:
Final preparations and training are completed and the plan is launched.

Step Ten:
Measurements are taken.

Pre-established measurements are taken. Debriefing meetings are held by the Executive Team and the Consultants to discuss the intended, as well as unintended consequences.

Step Eleven:
Feedback is given and the Master Plan is adjusted.

Feedback is given to the participants in the new efforts, particularly the Staff Leader and Ministry Leaders involved. The Master Plan is adjusted accordingly if the revised plans were not included in the year of implementation.

Methods

In many church Organizations, the one thing that should be given last consideration is often not only given first consideration, but top priority in terms of the identity and projection of ministry into the communities surrounding them. Two terms can be used to describe their identities.

Traditions

Traditions sometimes spring from theologies, but more often are a collection of attitudes that create a specific culture giving each church a certain identifiable uniqueness. Examples of what a community might say about a church's traditions include these.

- They serve communion every week.
- They dunk their believers under water.
- They have a great food and clothing pantry.
- They have a great choir.

Traditions are those characteristics that the community recognizes, even if the church possessing them does not and they are not always positive. They may include these examples of community perceptions.

- They are cliquish.
- They are cold.
- They preach that hell is hot and a lot of people are going there.

Regardless, most churches have some traditions which, for better or worse, become their identifying marks.

Programs

Programs are the ongoing recognizable efforts to facilitate the mission and vision of a local congregation. When programs never or seldom change, the community around a given church see them as its identifiers. Examples could include these possible identifiers.

- They host a terrific VBS every summer.
- They have an awesome kids worship program every Sunday morning.
- They give Christmas presents to needy families every year.
- They host great contemporary worship services on Sunday mornings.
- They have Bible studies during the week.
- They have men's and/or women's ministries.

There is nothing inherently wrong with programs. Their existence as the identifiable attributes of a given congregation at times may, however, be mistakenly substituted for the church's stated mission.

When sustaining traditions and programs becomes the chief concern of a church, those traditions and programs tend to sap the church of its power to accomplish anything else. Finances, human capital, building spaces, and hours spent by paid staff are devoted to assuring that these two kinds of community calling cards are maintained, many times to the detriment of any other efforts of the church. This can lead to the point that the success of the church begins to be measured by the numbers of people involved in sustaining these efforts as well as those benefiting from those efforts.

To expand your thinking, consider this example. There are churches who have an established program that annually suspends everything going on at their typical gathering place to instead go out into their community and "be the church." There is nothing wrong with doing this, but it begs the question of what they are doing on a regular basis with all the other days of the week. It's time for all churches to ask themselves, given the opportunity to choose to be known by any given set of identifiable characteristics, what those characteristics would be. Only after answering this question can traditions and programs find their rightful places in a church culture.

It's quite possible that a complete paradigm shift regarding who and what the church is and does is overdue, dramatically reducing the need for sustaining programs and traditions. If the church could see its existence as one recognized more by what is accomplished away from its buildings and outside the time frames of its gatherings, its ability to maximize its efforts would actually increase. Its need to prop up programming and extend its traditions would become less than necessary. These are important considerations when evaluating methods.

- The church must incorporate an 'all things to all people in order to save some' philosophy. Methods should remain flexible, changeable, even replaceable based on their ability to mobilize the Organization to speak love to The Boss. As the Master Plan is developed each year, it should reflect the leadership of The Boss in the changes to its programs.

Ministry Leaders should be allowed to use their gifting to propose programs that give the Organization its best opportunity to speak the Six Love Languages. Innovation should be seen as the discovery of new ways to make new disciples.

- When the Executive Team recognizes the need for new programming to revitalize or renew the health of the Organization, they should allow existing Ministry Leaders to utilize a variety of the Skills Not Typically Taught to find new people, ideas, and concepts to initiate new programming that better serves the needs of the Organization. (See Chapter 14, Page 161.) This should help the church avoid traps, such as "We've always done it this way," or "We've never done it that way before!" These traps prohibit the church from following the directions coming from The Boss.

- Avoid duplicating existing efforts and be fearless about borrowing good ideas from others. If someone in your community is already achieving success in an area of ministry in which your Organization is either weak or uninvolved, support the existing ministry, rather than duplicating it. If no one in your area is accomplishing something you know would help your congregation speak love to The Boss more fully, be fearless about investigation efforts being made by other churches in communities both near and far. In this way, the methods and programming in any given congregation will be supportive and innovative at the same time.

- Choose purpose over promotion. When new programs are initiated, they create excitement and enthusiasm naturally. It is critical that this passion be channeled into the accomplishment of the purpose of the program and into its success. The tendency is to over-promote new programs, rather than spending adequate time to assure that they hit a specific target. When new programs do not accomplish their purposes or hit their targets, this causes the enthusiasm and passion to quickly leave the ministry effort. Always remember that success breeds success and failure breeds failure. People do not quickly forget failed programs. It's always better to start small with extensive training, very little fanfare, and a low risk of failure, then build on success, rather than to heavily promote a new program that misses its intended mark and fails.

- Never prop up an old program simply for the sake of continuing a tradition. When a program has outlived its value to the Organization, attempting to sustain it can be detrimental in deeper ways than might first be realized. It exhausts volunteers, wastes resources, and distances the program from its perceived purpose and connection to speaking love to The Boss. It teaches the congregation that programs take priority over the leadership of

The Boss. When assembling the Master Plan each year, it is important to search each plan for its goals, fresh approaches and direct connection to speaking love to The Boss.

There are areas of church methods that need deliberate focus and strategic thinking but these are often overlooked by leaders who deem them extrabiblical or too much like corporate business thinking. How strategic and deliberate do you think Jesus was during the three and half years of His ministry?

In some Organizations these thoughts will turn into programs while in others, they will need to be incorporated into the culture. In any case, the leadership team, whether Ministry Leaders, Staff Leaders, the Executive Team, or a combination or cross section of the people; these areas require focus.

- Each church must decide the face they will present to the culture around them. This decision is a result of three factors of consideration.
  - » The culture, served by the Organization and from which it will derive its growth, will be a major contributor to this decision. Is the church in an urban, suburban, or rural setting? Is the predominate demographic younger, older, ethnically mixed, agricultural, industrial, or affluent? What communication channels will reach this culture best?
  - » What will differentiate this ministry from those around it? Unfortunately, people these days make interesting and unique choices regarding their

involvement in church. It used to be that theologies, denominational affiliations, and location would dictate where people would involve themselves in church, but not so much anymore.

Each church must decide how it will present itself to the communities they serve. It is a mistake to copy successful churches in your area to compete for church members. It is not a mistake to decide what will make your ministry unique among them.

This decision can evolve from the emphasis the church gives a specific ministry effort, such as, "We are great with kids! We change family lives by equipping parents to be spiritual leaders in their homes. We are a soul-winning church and train our people in a certain method of evangelism. We sing gospel music exclusively in our worship services!"

» How much media presence is necessary to expose us to the community around us? What will our logos, literature, brochures, etc. look like to match the other factors we've chosen? What information needs to be available on a website? Do we need an app? Do we need to live stream our services? Do we need an online bookstore, or YouTube channel?

There may be other discussions that may result from these three factors, but this is an area where strategic thinking needs to take place.

- Each church must develop for itself a critical path that leads a person from visitor to full involvement. This may include a path from unconverted to converted and involve a plan of salvation or at least a model for regeneration in response to the gospel. Many churches fail to grow because there is no clear path for visitors to follow into measurable involvement. There need to be multiple entry points into the path because visitors do not all follow each other through the same door into a church. Visitors may start in a Sunday morning worship service, by attending a special program at Christmas or Easter, by participating in a mid-week Bible Study, or joining a Home Cell Group. In any case, the steps to follow must be clear to the Organization, as well as to the visitor! This requires strategic thinking, which may result in a need for the oversight of a Ministry Leader.

- Every church must think through the inclusion factor, which results in discussions of style versus substance. The substance of the purpose and mission of the church never changes. Its purpose is to speak the Six Love Languages to The Boss and its mission is to make disciples.

  For the sake of inclusion, style must be discussed. No visitor, regardless of their differences, should be made to feel uncomfortable when present in a meeting of the family of God. It is important for each body of believers to be open to anyone, at any stage in life, in any predicament of life to understand that they are loved when they come into the circle of a group of people at church.

  To accomplish this, training may be necessary to break barriers in hearts and prepare attitudes. The subject of style may also lead to discussions and decisions regarding building décor, lighting effects, icons, seating arrangements, worship flow with internal summaries and transitional statements made during services, and appropriate dress for preachers and worship leaders.

- A mechanism and strategy for moving the church out from behind its walls merits significant consideration. To be successful, the church must accomplish more than simply being a pleasant place to worship on Sundays. The church must think of itself as an agent for change in the way its families function. It must invade its family cultures to be truly effective. Each church must decide how it will reduce the divorce rate among its married couples from the cultural norms that surround it, as well as training parents to raise children who walk with God from the earliest years of their lives. Each church must figure out a way to be relevant seven days a week, rather than simply on Sundays. This requires significant forethought and measurable intentionality.

- Every church must find a way to expose and celebrate the successes of its ministry efforts with every other part of the Organization. There are two scriptural concepts that support this idea. First,
    » Romans 12 teaches that each ministry gift, and those who utilize each one, belong to all the others.
    » I Thessalonians, as well as Romans 12 and other passages, teach us to encourage each other as we minister together.

Each church must find ways to communicate its successes to its members. Whether in newsletters, in short video clips played during worship services, by online blogs, by presentations to particular groups of seniors or leadership teams, success needs to be celebrated and encouragement freely shared. Too often, Christian saints labor in obscurity holding babies, teaching children, visiting nursing homes, or delivering help and hope to impoverished people without notice or encouragement by the rest of the Body of Christ, simply because no one exposed their work to the rest of the group.

CHAPTER 12

John's Accountability Model
for Intimacy with God
and Preparation for evangelism

Church leaders have often either ignored or brow beat their members in two regards without offering them a model for success. These two disciplines should be as common among the members of the church as eating and breathing are to the health of their bodies, but most churches seem to lack a model for teaching them.

- Developing personal intimacy with God
- Sharing the good news about Jesus with those who need to hear it

We have treated these two disciplines as if any given church member either gets it, or they don't. Church leaders have provided them with books on the subjects and held training classes for them, expecting them to succeed from those sources. In the most successful of churches, you will still typically find very limited numbers of members who are equipped and diligent enough to succeed in these two areas of their walk with Jesus. Tolerating this condition in the church is anathema.

When God made Adam and Eve in His own image, He did so for a specific purpose. He wanted them to be enough like Himself that they could walk with Him and receive His love while in their own ways loving Him back. The Garden of Eden was designed for intimacy between God and mankind. In biblical descriptions of heaven, it is easy to discover many similarities between the Garden of Eden and security of heaven.

Both are places to walk and eat together, have rivers running through them and fruit bearing trees growing in them, and are safe and secure. When God sets up the circumstances of life, He does so with maximum intimacy with the children He has created and recreated in mind.

- *The church needs to be a place where people can regain intimacy with God.*

  Intimacy with God changes people's perspectives on just about every aspect of their lives. Jesus came not only to free us from our sins, but to restore our relationship with God and to restore our intimacy with Him! To achieve maximum intimacy with God, the church needs a model that works, is simple, and lets experience be the teacher.

- *The church needs to be a place where every member can learn to share the gospel with others.*

  No member of the church should live in the kind of fear and intimidation that most do regarding a method or means of telling others about Jesus. The kinds of books and classes historically used for training have done little to get people past their fears and, in many cases, have created more phobias than they've eliminated. Small groups of soul winners have become the standard for evangelism in many congregations. The church needs to be a safe environment for all its members to learn how to share the difference Jesus has made in their lives with others. We need a model that works, is simple, and allows experience to be the teacher!

How do these two disciplines relate to each other? They may seem like altogether different subjects, and in most churches they are treated that way only making the problems developing each even greater. If we only had a model that combined the two disciplines and made the learning process easy, we could overcome two of the major inadequacies of most churches.

John's Accountability Model

My model is based on partnership between any two members of the Organization. Two people meet for 45 minutes once each week for six weeks at any convenient time and place upon which they can agree. It actually enhances the experience to find unique times and places. I have met early, late, and in the middle of the day. I have met in barns, taverns, sheds, kitchens, and even my office!

The more unique the place and time, the more unique and memorable the experience. At each meeting, the partners agree to share their experiences with God from the previous week. They do this by keeping a journal of their experiences in these five areas.

- Praise
- Prayer
- Memorization
- Introspection
- Stewardship

These five areas of intimacy are developed from the activities about which Jesus spoke in Matthew 6 when He was calling out the religious leaders for their hypocrisies of praying, fasting, and giving. Jesus intends these activities to be ones shared between God and His people without being noticed by anyone else. What takes place between the partners at their meetings is accountability and openness about their walks with God. Each person keeps a record, a journal, about what has been going on between themselves and God where no one else sees. They share openly with each other from their notes, taking turns until they cover all five.

Praise

Two things to note in this area are prompting and expression.

- Prompting

  Prompting to praise can come from many sources, such as a part of creation noticed, an activity of God in life, a scripture promise fulfilled, a prayer answered, a fruit of the Spirit born, or an encouraging word given or received. The list is virtually endless. The only requirement is awareness, an awareness that God can be noticed in hundreds of ways for Who He is and what He has done all around us all the time. Taking notice of God sensitizes intimacy with Him.

- Expression
  Praise is never passive in scripture. Thinking about praise doesn't qualify as praise. It must be expressed to be real. Each partner must note how the expression takes place. A few examples could be that a song is sung, knees are bent, hands are raised, a shout of joy is released, a tear is shed, a body is laid prostrate, a litany is whispered in the night, or a poem is written. At each meeting, the partners share with each other the prompting and the expression for their moments of praise from the previous week.

Prayer

Two components are noted here, as well.

- Intercessory Prayers
  What concerns or burdens is one carrying for others? Which of these need to be released to God's control for His wisdom to act and power to effect? Some of these concerns may be family, church leaders, our President, circumstances, relationships, healings, spiritual strengthening, decision- making, and preaching. Each partner shares their intercessory areas of prayer with their counterpart.

- Personal Prayers

  These prayers often convey concerns about relationships, the need for better choices about health, decisions about jobs, sensitivity to the Holy Spirit's work, commitment to promises, or delivery from temptation. The intimacy created between a person and God is directly related to his or her willingness to allow Him into every facet of their life, every corner of their heart, and every kingdom of their world. Prayer is the expression and emptying out of one's heart to God. These prayer thoughts are collected each week and shared between the partners.

Memorization

The partners must agree to memorize a section of scripture each week, which at their meetings they quote to each other. Scripture is God's most powerful way for telling us about Himself and teaching us our own value and purpose in the world. Memorizing it places it into our minds and hearts where His Spirit can work with us. The biggest difficulty in accomplishing this task is the volume chosen.

For this accountability model to succeed, the effort necessary must be achievable. If one partner has only enough time to memorize one verse per week, that is fine! At the end of the accountability period, they will have memorized six verses more than they knew at the beginning! If a partner can do more than one verse per week, great. The key is that each partner is packing the Word of God in his heart. The more we get to know God and His will for us, the more intimate with Him we become!

Introspection

I used to call this area meditation or reflection, but those words have meanings attached to them that can distract from the critical focus of this discipline. Introspection is the art of learning to listen to yourself and God at the same time. The Bible teaches that God's Spirit will work with or minister to our spirits. At some point, every Christian needs to be still and let God make character changes in His child. That's the point of introspection, an internal reflection on the events of one's life, allowing God to speak His will into each one.

Applying each of the fruits of the Spirit to the events of the day while allowing God to offer suggested changes to our behaviors or responses is not a cosmic event, just simple introspection. Notes are taken by each partner regarding the convictions felt about character changes God has in mind for them during the previous week and these convictions are shared at each meeting.

Stewardship

Every intimate relationship can be characterized by the contributions two people make to their shared values and priorities. Intimacy grows as they accomplish things together, with both making investments. The church has often reduced its teaching on stewardship to the level of paying dues or taxes. That is a mistake. Stewardship needs to be seen as partnership advancing the causes that are of greatest concern to God. He contributes. We contribute. In doing so, intimacy between us grows.

In our model, each person makes notes on the things they have done in partnership with God. It may be as simple as a smile, an encouraging word given, a gift given, time spent, a lesson taught, or a service rendered. The moment may come in ways unexpected until God prompts us to get involved with Him in one of the adventures of our lives. Having taken notes, each accountability partner shares from the moments of the previous week.

Final Follow Up Meeting

Following the sharing from their notes in these five areas of each person's journey each week, each prays for the other very specifically and the meeting concludes. At the sixth and final meeting of the accountability partners, an agreement is made and a promise given. The partners agree to pray a specific prayer for themselves and each other every day for the next six weeks. "God, show me and my partner the opportunities You have in mind for us to share the difference You are making in our lives with other people. Make it painfully obvious to us. Give us courage to share the Good News with them when You answer our prayers."

At this final meeting, a commitment is made between the partners, that if the Holy Spirit convicts either of them of their need to share the gospel with someone, they'll do it. They will not ignore the opportunities that God gives them.

In this way, intimacy and evangelism work together! Without realizing it, the accountability partners have not only increased their intimacy with God, but they have been preparing for the opportunities for which they will be praying. Each week, they have been verbalizing the exact things they need to say when someone needing the good news of Jesus opens themselves as answers to the prayers for such an opportunity.

When the Holy Spirit prompts an individual to share the gospel with someone, the first things to say are typically the most intimidating and fearful. By first practicing them for six weeks in a friendly environment, any church member should feel prepared to share.

To make the conversation easy to begin, the partners should ask a version of this question, "Do you have a few minutes for me to share with you the difference God is making in my life?" If the answer to this question is, "No," then the relationship continues, and no damage is done. If the answer is yes, then the sharing begins with five statements of testimony.

- God gives me Someone to thank for every good thing in my life.
- God gives me Someone to talk to 24 hours a day and night, 7 days a week. Whenever I call on Him, He listens. He is the One I talk to about everything.
- God gives me clear instruction about life. He tells me my purpose and the way to know I am happiest with what I am doing. His Word tells me just what I need to know.
- God makes me into a much better person than I otherwise would be. I am at peace with myself and what I say and do because His Spirit transforms me.
- God accepts everything I do to please Him. He and I partner to make the world a better place constantly.

The five areas of intimacy practiced for the previous six weeks can be brought to mind without hesitation! Additionally, if the person being spoken to asks for details, the journal is filled with all the details!

Each of the five statements of testimony is then followed with a question.

- Do you have a friend who you can thank for every good thing in your life?
- Do you have a friend who you can talk to at any time, and they'll always listen?
- Do you have a friend who always gives you the right advice about how to handle your life?
- Do you have a friend who turns you into a better version of yourself?
- Do you have a friend who will accept any effort you make to please him?

If the answer to these questions are "Yes," no damage is done and the relationship continues, but if it is, "No," then this follow up question is asked. "Would you like to learn about Jesus, God's Son, who is the Key to this whole thing?" Assuming the response is positive, hand the person a pocket copy of the Gospel of John and offer to read it with them. If there is no time for that, give them the copy and ask them to read it on their own. As they read, instruct them to highlight or underline every statement about Jesus or by Jesus that is used to identify Who He is. Agree to meet again, within one week, if possible.

After reading the Book of John together, or at the next meeting, ask this person to review all the highlighted or underlined places in their book then tell them, "That is Who

Jesus wants to be for you!" If their response to this is positive, read John 3:16 to them letting them know that in response to their desire to make Jesus Lord of their life, they should obey God's Word. Although your church may teach various ways to respond to the gospel, even a cursory review of biblical texts on the subject would include faith, repentance, confession, and baptism.

Assuming they respond, in this exuberant state of mind and heart, what should be done for this new convert? You should ask if they would agree to meet with you once each week, for the next six weeks, for 45 minutes each time, so you can teach them how to be intimate with God! So, on and on the process goes!

The Rules for Accountability Partnerships

- Males with males, and females with females, except between married couples.
- During the 45-minute meetings, conversations are restricted to the five elements of praise, prayer, memorization, introspection, and stewardship. Discussions about the church, life's problems, the weather, the Cubs, or anything else are kept out of the six meetings and can be discussed at other times and places.
- After six meetings, take a break, even if there is a desire to continue. Later on, another six-week partnership can be scheduled with the same partner.
- Journal notes do not need to be extensive. Many times, they will fit on one page. This process must be kept

simple to succeed; therefore, notes are collected weekly, not daily.

- If interruptions occur during the six-week schedule, make them up until all six meetings have taken place.

It is important to understand how this process fits into the management structure of the church. IT DOESN'T! This Accountability Model is not a program. It is not confined to or by any given layer of the Org Chart. It is not a role that is cast on one segment of the Organization. It does not need to be tracked. It can and should be promoted by those who have undergone it and allowed to spread through the church like yeast through dough. It will need champions who will begin it again and again no matter what the outcome. This will probably come from among the leadership, although it will succeed with anyone passionate about increasing their intimacy with God. When picking partners, those with experience should look to partner with those with less experience.

If not this accountability model, every church needs a model that accomplishes the two goals set forth in this one, which are increasing intimacy with God and preparing people to share the difference Jesus is making in their day by day lives with a world waiting to hear the good news about Jesus.

CHAPTER 13
Uncharted Territories

There are areas of church management that must be addressed but are not called out by specific processes or layers on the Org Chart. They exist as either cultural factors or leadership precepts but are critical to the success of the Organization. I've called them Uncharted Territories because they do not fit on the Org Chart. They represent areas where churches struggle even to discuss them as they evoke discussions that devolve quickly into unending theological debates. These topics become contentious because they relate to power and control. All of them need a way to be addressed rationally and in line with the thinking of The Boss. This book is about management, not theology; therefore, the goal is to offer concepts and principles that can be considered by churches of any theological stripe.

Roles for Women

The best list of functional gifts for the church is recorded in Romans 12. There are other lists of gifts in scripture, but Paul's list in Romans 12:3-8 is specified as a list of the Body's functional gifts, which relates directly to the management and functionality of the church. It is interesting to note two factors about these seven gifts.

- **These gifts are given to converts as a matter of grace.**

   When the Holy Spirit is planted into the heart of the penitent sinner at conversion, along with Him comes functional gifting. The Boss connects with converts not only to save them and create intimacy with them, but to give them a function in the Organization and no one gets left out. Every convert receives at least one of these seven gifts as a matter of grace.

- **These gifts are not gender specific.**

   Nothing about the list indicates that males receive certain gifts unavailable to females. The reverse is true as well. It appears that The Boss has in mind what He wants from the members of His Body and empowers them to accomplish it when He makes His home in them, regardless of their gender. The list is preceded by the cautionary statement that no one is to think more highly of themselves than they should when soberly considering what conversion has accomplished for them.

   The Boss's choice about who gets which gifts should

never create schisms in the Organization. His choices are to give every church the functionality it needs to accomplish His work, and gender does not appear to be a consideration in His decision-making. Anyone denying a woman the privilege of using a gift given to her by The Boss amounts to insubordination, an offense most corporate bosses would consider untenable.

The List of Gifts in Romans 12

- Prophesying
- Serving
- Teaching
- Encouraging
- Giving
- Leading
- Showing Mercy

There should be no layer on the Org Chart where females should be made to feel uncomfortable functioning in any of these seven ways. The functionality of these gifts is necessary in every layer of the Org Chart. Restricting God-given functionality in the church is to work against the functionality The Boss has deliberately placed into His Organization. Evangelism becomes one of discovering gifts and providing opportunities for their functionality regardless of gender, rather than the privilege of a few men assigning gifts to various parts of the Organization based on gender.

For churches whose theologies, traditions, or doctrines exclude women from certain prophesying (preaching), teaching, or leadership roles, consider the following points.

- Whether or not you restrict women from certain titles or ordinations on your staff, do not hesitate to hire women and utilize them, treating them as functional equals with all other staff members.
- Find creative ways to allow women to address the congregation. If standing behind the pulpit is a problem, remove your pulpit. If making women the leaders of discussions in Life Groups or Sunday School Classes is acceptable nomenclature, then let them teach.
- Invite women to the meetings of the eldership or church board to serve as consultants if having women on either of those counsels is a problem for your church. There is no theological reason their thoughts should be excluded from the consideration of any official board.
- Eliminate roles that have traditional gender bias built into them or begin utilizing women in those roles alongside your men. These can include opportunities for serving communion, collecting offerings, making announcements, leading worship, coordinating events, or calling in hospitals and homes.

I am not a scholar, but from my studies it has become apparent to me that supporting slavery as a biblical theology is more easily accomplished than defending the historical and traditional treatment of women in the church. During the American Civil War both the North and South thought God was on their side! When the church came to grips with the errors of its thinking about slavery, there occurred a great repentance in churches all over America. It may very well be time for the church to undergo another moment of repentance regarding the dignity of women and the roles they are gifted to assume in the church.

Theologies and Membership

The church has made one of its most grave mistakes by becoming the broker of the real estate of the kingdom of God. We have divided up the Body of Christ by our theological understandings of who is in and who is out of the kingdom. We assign particular places of worship and fellowship to believers of each of the conclusions we have drawn about the plan of salvation. Ironically, these divisions have been made to honor our Savior who spent some of the final hours of His life on earth praying that all believers, everywhere would remain one!

Those same conclusions are used to make rules determining who is allowed to be an official voting member of any given local congregation. Rules of this kind do not appear in scripture, but we create by-laws and church constitutions to explain their implementation. This creates theological and local wickets through which a newcomer must navigate as they seek a path to involvement in the local Organization, and if this newcomer moves to a new locale, the rules will likely change!

It is little wonder that unchurched people struggle to find the critical path to assimilation and incorporation into a local church. The membership rules change along with certain theologies, which cause them to question their salvation every time they walk through the doors of a different church.

I offer this suggestion to every stripe and denomination of church no matter the conclusions that have been drawn concerning when regeneration takes place in the life of a penitent sinner. Simply open the book of Acts and have your newcomers respond to the gospel the same way the converts of the early church did. No need to complicate it any further than that. Acts chronicles the earliest conversions and additions to the church, as well as exactly how that process occurred as the church was birthed into the world.

This allows you to make one rule about church membership. It is open to anyone who has responded to the call of the gospel. May I offer a set of principles by which you can differentiate who is in and who is out of the kingdom, and the local church?

Theologies and subsequent rules about church membership are established from various scripture texts drawn out of differing contexts. This explains why so many different churches can come to so many conclusions about the subject. If we can't find one author in scripture who is speaking specifically and directly to the subject of who is in and who is out of the church, then the safest way to address this subject is to keep silent about it. Fortunately, there is one author who, because of certain heresies making their way into the teachings of some first century churches, addresses the issue head on. In the epistles of I and II John, John made three assertions.

- Members of the true church must acknowledge that Jesus is the Messiah, the Savior of the world, the only means of the forgiveness of sin, and the only way to a restored relationship with God.
- Members of the true church must exhibit a spirit of obedience to everything Jesus taught about His kingdom, not choosing from parts of His teaching and filling in the rest with their own constructs
- Members of the true church must love each other.

With these assertions firmly stated, John clearly establishes the grounds on which people can be considered in or out of the church. He then inextricably links them to each other so that a person can never claim one without also claiming the other two. A church can teach whatever model or tradition it claims regarding the process of salvation or regeneration, but as for church membership, these three principles remain the best for teaching newcomers who is in and who is out!

Worship Music and Praise

I can recall times when the choir room of the church was affectionately referred to as the war room! Not many churches have dedicated rooms for rehearsing choirs anymore, but the wars still rage, quite possibly with greater devastation than ever before. The battlefields tend to be those of control and style. Since we have established that the goals for speaking the language of adoration are authenticity, expression, and passion many issues about music and praise in worship can be easily addressed.

- It is more critical that the church sings with one voice, one energy, and one mind and heart than it is to have a well-liked style of music in a worship service. The style of music offers people the opportunity to connect their hearts and minds with their voices so they can worship in spirit and truth. Whether a traditional, blended, or contemporary style, it fails if people fail to use it to effectively praise the audience of all worship, God, Who is the audience of One!

  There will always be people who prefer one style of music over another. The selection process must be influenced most by how well the music achieves authenticity, expression, and passion in the hearts of the worshippers. Visitors to a worship service will notice whether the members freely, openly, and passionately worship God more readily than whether they approve of the style of music being utilized.

- We are given wide latitude regarding style from New Testament scripture. Choices of style are guided by the three forms of psalms, hymns, and spiritual songs. People must be taught to understand these forms and use them for their connection to worship in spirit and truth. Teach with words and experiences. Talking about worship informs the teaching while practical experience confirms it. Teach a little. Experience a little. Then teach and experience a little more. Work to build latitude of mind and heart in the people regarding various approaches to worshiping God. Changes should not be made until the people are taught how they can connect with the change as they authentically and passionately express their praise to God.

- Recognize that all music since the time of King David has been contemporary music! Many people do not understand the history of worship music and how long it's been contemporary. Every generation for centuries has had its own musical style, a truth about which many people are ignorant. In the last 700 years, musical forms, rules, and sounds have been revised perpetually. Chants, medieval, renaissance, baroque, classical, romantic, modern, and post-modern represent a progression. As the church has incorporated these styles, moving from one musical form to the next across the years, there has been no small upheaval by musicians and worshippers during the transitions!

  People relate to the musical style of their own era and have difficulty adjusting to new forms when subsequent generations are drawn to their own styles. At some point in history, it would be nice if, instead of rebelling against these natural progressions, people could recognize and allow them for the sake of the deeper truths that would demonstrate devotion to God, to each other, and to the world.

- Worship leaders must understand that authenticity, expression, and passion begin with them. If a worship leader believes that musicianship or performance is more important than those three criteria, either retrain or replace them. If any part of the Executive Team or Staff Leadership believes in performance over authenticity, teach them otherwise. All levels of leadership must see that worship in spirit and truth is not optional but required!

Decision-Making and Communication

Few things cripple the credibility of leaders faster than indecisiveness and lack of communication. Ministry Leaders must do both well. Staff Leaders must do both even better than Ministry Leaders. Executive Team members must do both the best of all! Sadly, churches often struggle in 30-day decision cycles in which decisions languish, and communication seldom leaks out of meeting rooms.

Although there is truth in the adage, "a bad decision is better than no decision," a timely and good decision, based on well-regarded principles and well-known processes is even better. Decision-making is simplified if a ministry effort is based on principles and priorities explained in advance in the Master Plan, and the work functions within the parameters of well-established processes.

If every decision made is effectively communicated to anyone involved in its implementation, the results, as measured by effective and contented workers, will be excellent.

Any decision not communicated, however good it may be, carries with it the potential to create more problems than it solves. Decisions and communication work hand in hand with each other and cannot be thought through apart from each other. Every decision-maker in the entire the Organization must think through not only the potential positive outcomes and negative ramifications of their decisions, as well as those to be told or trained to implement the decision.

Decision-making authority in the church must not be controlled by people, but by the Master Plan. When Ministry Leaders submit their plans each year, they must recognize the freedom and obligation to work within them. Any decision that needs to be made to keep a plan on track must be given to the Ministry Leader running it. Any decision that either alters the plan or affects another ministry's ability to successfully continue with its plans, must include the Staff Leaders and Ministry Leaders affected by it. This includes staying within budgets approved for every ministry functioning as a part of the Master Plan.

Three principles of decision-making and communicating will free Ministry Leaders and involve those necessary for decisions to be both effective and well- communicated.

Principle One

If a decision affects only the volunteers and leaders directly involved in a ministry included in the Master Plan, the Ministry Leader should make that decision and communicate it to their ministry team. These decisions can and should be made as quickly as they are necessary. Backing away from them will only undercut the credibility of the leader who must be willing to take responsibility for any negative ramifications, as well as pride in any positive outcome.

Principle Two

If a decision affects other Ministry Leaders and their functions, discussions must include those Ministry Leaders before the decision is made. The Staff Leaders supporting those Ministry Leaders should also be involved. Making decisions that affect other ministries without including them in the discussion demonstrates a lack of respect and can create unnecessary ill will, even rivalry, between ministries and their leaders.

Principle Three

If a decision could affect the vision or direction of the entire Organization, a process should be followed.

1. Offer the idea (not the plan) to the Executive Team and Staff Leaders for consideration. This idea should be allowed to germinate with these two groups for an established period of time.
2. Objections and questions regarding the implementation of the idea must be met and answered before a plan is put forward.
3. Present the idea to the Ministry Leaders for their input.
4. Inform the congregation.
5. Develop and communicate the plan to the entire Organization. Only then can there be a decision to implement the plan. Significant training or other

logistics may be involved in this implementation; therefore, a broad scope of communication is imperative.

Any decision that may require modifications or renovations to buildings or equipment should be overseen by Ministry Leaders designated for the tasks of monitoring and maintaining buildings and grounds.

Church Boards

Since church boards have few, if any, equivalencies in scripture, they are noticeably absent from the Org Chart in this book. The usefulness of a church board as a management entity is limited. Although church boards carry with them both strengths and weaknesses, many churches have found the weaknesses to be great enough to discontinue their use. Boards often do more to satisfy the laws of the state, in order for the church to be able to claim not-for-profit status, than they actually contribute to the ministry efforts of the local church.

Strengths of Church Boards
- Their meetings act as mini congregational meetings where important information about vision and methods can be shared in advance of plans. In this way Ministry Leaders can take the pulse of the congregation prior to executing plans. Since the constituencies of most church boards are elders, deacons, and trustees they tend to rep-

resent the spiritual and financial backbone of the congregation.

- Board members often represent years of investment in the congregation and their decisions meet with quick approval by the older members of the congregation. The board's approval of any idea typically makes it palatable to the majority of the longest standing members of the Organization.

- Church board members can serve as liaisons between the staff, elders, and congregation when they are kept well-informed. They can also help to suppress rumors and quell gossip when they are given timely and accurate information.

Weaknesses of Church Boards

- Dissention forms and factions develop when Board members are allowed to express their approval or disapproval on issues by voting. If members are not trained to come into meetings as representatives and leave as ambassadors, they can be the authors of discord. Phrases like, "I didn't vote for that," when expressed by board members tend to be divisive.

- Board members can use their positions on the board as an influence even when they are uninvolved in programming. This amounts to pulling rank in areas where they have little or no investment.

- If the church must have the approval of its board for nearly every decision made, it can undercut the decisions of smaller groups of decision-makers up to and including the Executive Team. This can put the Executive Team in a mode of fear, instead of confidence as they strive to follow the leading of The Boss.

- Typically, church boards meet once a month which elongates the decision- making cycle unnecessarily.

The Unwritten Code of Conduct

In the bottom three layers of the Org Chart, there should exist an adherence demanded to an unwritten code of conduct. Everyone working in these layers should give their firm commitment and allegiance to this code. The code is justified by one verse of scripture that the church has glossed over far too long.

"Do not let any unwholesome talk come out of your mouths, but only what is helpful for building others up according to their needs, that it may benefit those who listen." Ephesians 4:29

Code of Conduct

We do not participate in conversations that may undercut any leader in this congregation.

1. The Code of Conduct gives every leader in the Organization the confidence and support they need to follow the direction of The Boss. They can make decisions, execute plans, recruit and train volunteers, even make mistakes with the understanding that no other leader in the Organization will talk to or listen to others talk negatively about them behind their back.
2. The Code of Conduct gives every leader permis-

sion to direct anyone in the Organization having an issue with another leader to talk to that leader. All leaders are responsible to end conversations wherever they may occur by pointing people back to the source of their concern.

3. The Code of Conduct gives every leader permission to step away from conversations saturated with gossip.

4. The Code of Conduct sets a measurable standard of ethics for the operation. When a leader breaks the code, other leaders should be empowered to approach that leader. If efforts to correct or restore the person in error are resisted, other leaders can be brought into the conversation. Ultimately, a breach of conduct and resistance to correction should be considered a performance issue and discipline applied.

This verse has handed the church the means of addressing gossip, one of its most divisive problems. We are overdue for the serious application of the principle set forth by it!

The Hiring Process

"Be slow to hire and quick to fire," is a concept that applies to the church even more than business, but unfortunately, the opposite tends to be the case historically. Churches tend to hang onto staff that have long since lost their value and usefulness to the Organization, then hire replacements based on the time a small group of people can devote to a process which is based more on impressions than real criteria and the direction of The Boss.

Second only to the annual Master Planning process should be the involvement of the entire congregation when hiring staff. A typical hiring process will include the following phases which should be considered mileposts in the understanding of the congregation. These mileposts should be kept transparent before the congregation on an ongoing basis, so they can be praying, fasting and seeking the leading of The Boss during each and every phase of the hiring process.

Hiring Phases

- The need for the new hire is presented to and approved by the congregation.
- A search team is selected and assembled representative of the congregation at large but including heavily invested people in the area of ministry in which the hew hire will work.
- Preliminary organizational meetings of the search team should be planned for the purpose of outlining and reviewing the process, agreeing to covenant terms, brainstorming, qualifying and prioritizing candidate criteria, formulating questionnaires for follow up, creating "no thank you" letters, selecting communication channels, developing a list of responsibilities, and bathing everything in prayer. Covenant terms should include complete confidentiality regarding search team deliberations.
- A solicitation phase is embarked upon where decisions are made, such as where postings will be placed, where

referrals through designated and qualified sources will be sought, what networking loops will be established, and how selection criteria will be advertised.

- A qualification phase ensues where applications and resumes are reviewed against established criteria, communication with candidates under consideration is ongoing, and letters of rejection are sent to unqualified candidates.
- A follow up phase takes place during which questionnaires are sent to candidates under consideration.
- An interview phase starts where candidates of interest are brought in for interviews, background checks are run, and skills are tested. Staff Leaders are included during this phase for their input regarding fitness to serve with existing staff.
- A recommendation phase occurs when a candidate is chosen and recommended to the Executive Team for approval.
- The completion phase is celebrated where the new hire is introduced to the congregation and orientation begins.

The congregation should be made aware as each new phase begins so they can focus their prayers for the search team as the process progresses. Hiring staff can be as celebratory as it can be contentious based on the amount of communication and information given to the congregation as the process unfolds.

There are several over-arching principles to bear in mind.

Hiring Principles

- Total transparency is essential with no political shenanigans, no quid pro quos, no hidden agendas, and no nepotism. Everything is kept in the open.
- Hiring is a two-way judgement. The candidate must be sold on the opportunity just as much as the search team is sold on the candidate. Keep that in mind when both advertising and interviewing.
- Leave no stone unturned. Talk to all references, find new references, and rely on references offered by existing staff. Test the skills as well as the spirit of the candidate.
- Bathe everything in prayer, during every phase, at every meeting, in every interview, and throughout every discussion. Seek to please The Boss, not the people!
- Keep everyone informed!

Roles for Deacons

Deacons are like knights in a game of chess. They aren't the king or queen, or even the rooks and bishops, but if there's a problem going on in the middle of the chess board, they are amazing assets to deploy to get a player out of trouble. Deacons perform two important functions for any layer on the Org Chart. They are problem-solvers and indefatigable workers. They get things done! Even so, the attributes in scripture that qualify them to serve in the role of deacon are almost exclusively about their spiritual maturity.

Wherever and whenever they work in the functionality of the Organization, they are an example anyone else can follow on their spiritual journey. Make no mistake. One of the best assets the Organization has at its disposal when getting things done whenever the need arises are its deacons.

There are two ways deacons find their place in the structure and functionality of the Organization.

- Deacons can make themselves available in a crisis.

    Our country has recently endured a pandemic. The deacons in every church should have been clamoring for opportunities to help people during this crisis asking, "Who can I help? Does anyone need groceries delivered? Can I pick prescriptions for some of our seniors? Is everyone's heat working? Does the staff at the church building have everything they need to be successful as the flow of their work changes?" That's the way deacons respond in tough times. They look to solve problems and serve in any way they can.

- Deacons find places where their gifts fit in the ongoing ministry efforts of the church.

    From the list of gifts in Romans 12, deacons know themselves well enough to be able to find an ongoing role in the Master Plan of the Organization. They get involved because it is their nature to dig in and help. It's who they are in their inner being.

Deacons historically run into difficulties when they assume that the title of Deacon gives them elevated authority in the Organization. A few examples of this include:

- They presume that they are qualified to change the course of a Ministry Leader's plan.
- They believe they have spiritual authority to correct behaviors of people who are not living their Christianity up their own personal standards.
- They consider that the title is really an office, and their role is only as a board member which entitles them to vote on the important issues of the church.

Deacons have occasionally demonstrated a unique creativity for inventing roles for themselves that neither appear in scripture or are helpful to the success of the Organization. Deacons are valuable assets when they understand how the management structure of the church works and exactly how they can plug in and help the Organization succeed! They should be trained to think of themselves in those terms.

Discovering Functional Gifts

It is interesting to observe churches who spend large amounts of time, effort and many times money to investigate the spiritual giftedness of their members. After having "discovered" their gifts, the vast majority of those members are simply offered the same places in the same programs as before their gifts were discovered. The opportunities afforded by the programming do not necessarily match any of the gifts from the list for which the tests were taken. People who can speak are asked to preach or teach. People who can sing are placed on praise teams. Those who can cook, cook. I've never seen public speaking, singing, or cooking on any list of functional gifts in scripture, so the outcome doesn't seem to correlate with the effort.

The list of functional gifts in Romans 12 exists to clarify what The Boss has in mind for the church through His eyes and His gifting, rather than regarding programs more highly than the gifts He has given to His followers. If God knows what He wants the church to accomplish in any given locale (and He does), and He gifts that church for success (and He does), then a close look at the correlation between the giftedness of the members and the programming planned is imperative. Gifting may have much more to do with the vision and direction of the church than many leaders may think. Discovering the giftedness of a congregation is significant, not merely to discover the capabilities and capacities of the members, but also to discover what The Boss has in mind to accomplish!

There exists a simple approach to the discovery process, which is easy to administer. It is an inexpensive alternative to the hours, effort, and expense of administering standardized tests or hiring consultants. Have the members read the following story and answer the subsequent questions.

If eight people are seated at the dining room table, each with a glass of milk, what do you suppose is bound to happen? You would be correct if you predicted that one person would spill their milk. When the glass of milk is overturned, you would probably see seven responses from the others seated at the table.

1. One person would probably stand and in a very loud voice announce to everyone in the house, and possibly the neighborhood, "You knucklehead! You spilled your milk!" It would be a loud declaration of the truth of the moment.

2. Without saying a word, another person at the table would jump up, run into the kitchen for the cleaning supplies, and grab (what my mom used to call) a hot soapy rag! That same person would go about cleaning up the table and the floor and might even pull the leaves of the table apart so that no milk could spoil in the cracks of the table.

3. There will definitely be one person who will begin explaining how it all happened, describing the position of the glass, the angle of the elbows at the table, and how all the events worked together to cause the spill. In vivid detail, everyone present would get an explanation.

4. Someone might leap from their seat and begin telling everyone that everything is going to be alright, running laps around the table, making sure that no one panics, and ensuring that everyone is at peace in the midst of the chaos.

5. Another person at the table might say, "That's okay. There's more milk in the refrigerator and glasses in the cupboard. In fact, if that's the last of the milk, I'll just run to the store and get some more."

6. Inevitably, another person at the table will halt the chaos for a moment saying, "Stop! Let's get organized! We've got one person hollering, another trying to clean up this mess, someone trying to explain everything, somebody else running laps around the table shouting that everything is okay, and someone headed out to buy more milk! We should get out of each other's way so everyone can contribute to the recovery we have going on here!"

7. The last person at the table might walk over to the person who spilled the milk and whisper, "Don't worry. We all spill our milk once in a while. No one is going to throw you out of this family just because you spilled a glass of milk."

After reading this account, have each of your members answer these questions.

- Which of the seven responses is most like what you would do if someone spilled a glass of milk at your table?
- If you had to rank the seven responses from most like you to least like you, how would you rank them?
- Which response of the seven do you think is the best response to the situation?

These seven responses correlate directly with the seven gifts of ministry found in Romans 12. A quick evaluation of the three answers to the questions listed above juxtaposed against the list of seven gifts in Romans 12 will reveal the probable giftedness of anyone reading the story and giving their answers. It's not rocket science!

1. Prophesying
2. Serving
3. Teaching
4. Encouraging
5. Giving
6. Leading
7. Showing Mercy

Everyone in the Organization should be taught the following principles about their giftedness.

- Don't wait for church programming to give you an opportunity to begin exercising your gift inside and outside the church. Your gifts are The Boss's blessing and directive for a lifestyle He has chosen for you. Live your gifts. Give the blessing of your giftedness away every day of your life.
- Recognize that others in the Organization may have similar gifts to yours. That works because The Boss knows how many people need to have the gifts He thinks are necessary to create success in the ministry of His church.
- Occasionally, you'll have to allow other people to give their gift to you because you may be the one who spills your milk! Receiving the gifts of others

may not come easily in your nature but be grateful for their gifts when the time comes.

- As Executive Team members examine the accumulated answers to questions, God will be telling much about the direction He wants the church to go, such as which ministries may need more focus or which ministries have no one gifted to carry them forward.

Teaching on Giving

I struggle to number the advertisements, email blasts, phone calls, and free books I've ignored over the course of the last eight years of my ministry each guaranteeing substantial increases in giving for the church I serve. It is hard to imagine what kingdom work might have been done with the dollars invested in these efforts. It would be staggering, I'm sure.

I also find it difficult to comprehend the 'give to get' mentality that floods the internet and TV programming. The church at large seems to be materializing the blessings of God and reducing them to some sort of quid pro quo between themselves and God. We are being taught to bargain with God for His blessing and His favor. This line of teaching is degrading to the nature of the kingdom described by Jesus in the blessings described in the Beatitudes (Matthew 5:1-12).

Giving, if it is to be non-compulsory, ungrudgingly, even cheerful, must be taught to members of the Organization as if it is as natural as breathing. Giving is one part of the Love Language of Partnership and is exactly how it should feel to a Christian when giving to God and His kingdom work, that the partnership is working, and that love is being expressed. Giving should be taught on three levels.

First Fruits Giving

Giving a designated portion of the bounty of what is produced by working on God's earth dates back to Abel, Noah, and Abraham. This concept was honed by the law given to Moses on Mt. Sinai when tithing was made a standard portion for first fruits giving.

This concept continued into the New Testament era and was supported by Jesus and Paul. Every person who walks with God and enjoys fruits from his/her labors should automatically respond, "I should give to God a portion of the first of what has come into my possession." Even if the gift is not a tithe, some portion of the best should go first to Him. Many parents teach their children with their allowance money that the first of it goes back to God from whose Hand it was given.

Need-Based Giving

Our target verses in Acts 2 and 4 describe giving in the early church as driven by needs. The need of one drove the sacrifice of another. There existed a sensitivity in the early church that wouldn't let people with basic needs go unattended. Every Christian should carry that passion with them in all of life's circumstances and should exist without prompting or compulsion.

When Moses put out the call for offerings, which were to provide the raw materials to construct the Tabernacle, the Bible tells us that the willing-hearted responded. No one was forced to give to meet the need and yet, the need was met. In fact, so much was given by the willing-hearted people that Moses had to restrain them from giving too much! It is this exact passion that should be trained into the mindset of the church. The people of the Organization must never see a need they are not willingly compelled to meet.

Moments of Extreme Generosity

Possibly only once in a lifetime, every Christian should experience a moment of extreme generosity when a prompting from the Holy Spirit compels the Christian to make an extreme sacrifice on behalf of someone else. It was the case when the widow gave her two copper coins, when Zacchaeus gave half of all he owned to the poor and paid back four times the amount he may have cheated anyone, and when the Macedonian churches gave with rich generosity out of their extreme poverty. It could have happened again had the rich young ruler found the passion for it in his heart.

It happens, when in an overpowering compulsion occurs in the heart of someone who goes beyond what seems reasonable to contribute to a cause they believe in. This level of extreme generosity should be taught to the congregation.

Teaching these three levels of giving to the church will make collecting offerings on Sundays a joyful, cheerful worship experience where no one feels as though they are paying taxes or dues. Some Sunday, encourage your members to verbalize their joy as they give their offering. Encourage them to shout out a praise or clap their hands. You won't believe how it will change the worship experience of giving in your service!

The Apprenticeship Model for Developing Leaders

One of the fundamental reasons for writing this book is to give the church a structure and description of basic functionality that can bridge the gaps when leaders leave, quit, retire, or pass away. Churches are often affected most by turn over in leadership and yet seem to be the least prepared for it. Statistics are plentiful regarding how staggeringly short the tenure of most vocational ministry people is in the typical church. It is incumbent upon the church to ready itself for these transitions, rather than going through the downturns and upheavals they notoriously cause.

Every Ministry Leader, Staff Leader, and Executive Team member should be mentoring a leader who could replace them should they vacate their role in the Organization. The approach to this process should be Rabbinic. Every leader finds a follower to train by working alongside them during every phase of planning and execution.

They should partner with an apprentice when answering the seven questions for the Master Plan, developing a budget, making decisions about programming, making changes to programming, when weekly programming occurs, and becoming partners to implement John's Accountability Model. Every leader should make training a new leader a part of their work. Doing a job is not their only responsibility, but training a replacement is also part of the job.

As it regards succession planning for vocational Staff Leaders or teaching minsters, a longer-term plan needs to be utilized. If the church's processes, planning methods, and management principles are firmly in place, succession is much easier to plan and execute. When possible, moving a successor onto the staff in another role to allow time for them to acclimate to and undergo indoctrination in these well-established methods is preferred.

The apprenticeship model is easily accomplished by serving on the staff together for a measure of time. This process demands significant humility on the part of the staff member who is being replaced. The church should avoid hiring any replacement who does not acknowledge and agree to maintain the existing management methods. If they are wise, most new hires in high profile roles would be thrilled to find management systems in place that they did not have to develop, fix, or replace. Succession plans can be executed over the course of two or three years if executed by humble leaders.

Many available methods or plans exist on the web, but these four principles should apply to any succession plan.

1. Promote total transparency. The entire Organization should remain informed about the plan for succession and the roles involved.
2. Allow more time than you might think is necessary. The good will that is developed in the Organization by two Spirit-led, humble leaders making a longer smooth transition has great value. The ill will that occurs when two egomaniacal leaders make a mess of a cut short transition can leave scars on the Organization that do not easily heal.

3. Determine the end from the beginning. Tell everyone either the calendar date, or measurable milepost that will end the transition.

4. Hiring from within can sometimes create nepotistic problems that can cause wounds in an Organization. If active, qualified people in any area of ministry demonstrate unique abilities and gifts to lead in place of a departing staff member, there are many unique advantages to hiring them. Handling this process with great transparency and considerable searching for The Boss's direction can lead to success.

Principles of Global Outreach

Nearly every church wants to think of itself as having global impact as it regards taking the gospel to places where it has never been preached. When making choices about whom to support, or where funds should be sent the following principles should be followed.

- The best missionaries to support are those who are well known to the Organization. To secure the prayers and financial support behind a distant ministry requires exposure and knowledge of those involved. Timothies of the congregation make great candidates for this.
- Supporting high impact, well known, existing missionary organizations cuts down on the amount of overhead

expense which is sometimes wasted in the attempt to initiate new ministry efforts from a distance. This requires significant investigation on the part of the Ministry Leader and team overseeing the global impact efforts of the church.

- Budgets developed for global impact ministries should be kept completely transparent to the Organization. Changes should be exposed before they are implemented.

- Nepotism must be kept out of the decision-making of the ministry team overseeing the global impact efforts. Not even a hint should be allowed. If members serving on the global impact team have a conflict of interest, they should either step off the team or recuse themselves from the applicable decisions as they are made.

- Supporting local ministries with global outreach is helpful. Significant investigation should be made regarding overhead and administrative costs, but once a church is satisfied with the efforts of the local ministry, constant contact and exposure are more easily maintained.

- Exposure, exposure, exposure! Keeping the names, faces, and results of global impact ministries supported by the congregation in their viewfinder is essential. Use every available media means to keep these ministries exposed to the Organization.

CHAPTER 14
Skills Not Typically Taught

It is baffling that the one Organization on earth with the greatest need for efficiency, urgency, and effectiveness is the one that teaches the skills necessary to produce these results the least. There exist proven skills which are not contrary to the movement and leadership of The Boss but are typically ignored by the church. That makes no sense to me. Why would we let businesses around us utilize success skills that we, simply because we do not (and should not) identify ourselves as businesses overlook?

Much of what follows could be considered life skills as easily as Organizational skills. Unless they have most recently radically altered their curriculum, I know of few, if any, ministry training colleges or universities that include these skills in their vocational ministry preparation. The unfortunate response of most church leadership teams is to wish their Ministry Leaders knew these skills but make little effort or take little time to teach them.

The outline that follows is just that, an outline. Many online resources are available to teach these skills in depth.

If you prefer books, check out the *50 Minute Book* series from Crisp Publications. These are basic principles to introduce their functionality to the Organization. These skills would typically be found in every layer of the Organization, but primarily in the Ministry Leader, Staff Leadership, and Executive Team layers. Such skills are critical in these layers for the success of the Organization.

Time Management

The Bible routinely emphasizes the brevity of life, describing it as a vapor and in other similar terms. To maximize what we are each given, intentionality or purposefulness must be considered for each of our days. Some sort of plan is essential to accomplish meaningful things, as well as to get a sense of accomplishment from each day.

Some people structure their days around "to do" lists and get a great satisfaction by crossing their accomplishments off the list as they are completed. Others like to consider themselves more organic or free-flowing and would consider themselves bound by such lists. Even the most spontaneous people benefit from outlining their intentions.

The key principle of daily time management is structure, a plan! Taking time at the beginning of each day to plan the events of the day will most certainly increase its productivity. After a plan is established, there are refinements that can be made to the plan.

Plan Refinements

Prioritization

There are ways to be active during a day without accomplishing anything meaningful. Knowing the difference between taking time for necessary activities, like eating and reserving time for progressive activities like learning or growing more intimate with The Boss is critical. A daily plan must consider both and must include both for success in the long run.

Positioning

Some necessary tasks fall naturally into particular parts of each day. For example, a person will probably eat three times at regular intervals every day. Many people are guilty of using their best energies on meaningless tasks. If you are a morning person with your most creative thoughts at the beginning of each day, why would you spend the opening minutes of each day opening emails, or answering text messages, then try to dream up new ideas for programming after lunch when you are tired and feel like napping? When you understand your unique flow of energy for each day, you can begin to plan the things you will do around the most appropriate times to do them.

Consolidation

It is surprising how much time each of us wastes each day by interruptions (most of which we create for ourselves). We get part way through one thing and then remember we need to do something else. As we begin to do that thing, we remember a third thing, and on and on it goes until our days pass and we wonder where time went. By grouping like tasks together, it's easier to stay on them until one set is done before beginning another.

Time Study

Put a notepad in your pocket and for one week, pause every fifteen minutes to jot down what you just did. After you do a personal time study, you'll be amazed at the changes you'll make in your daily planning as you look back at the things you did as opposed to the things you could have done.

One final note about time management is respect for other people's time. Don't be the last or consistently late person to meetings. Don't digress in either meetings or conversations. Show respect for the daily plans of others with whom you interact each day.

Meeting Management

No matter how simple we may want to organize the structure of the church, it will always be necessary for groups of people to meet to make things happen. Unfortunately, most churches have earned a reputation for meetings that last too long and get very little accomplished. As infrequently as members of our Organization can and do make themselves available for meetings, many things get put off to a point of irrelevancy. Learning to plan and execute effective meetings is a skill well worth mastering for our Organization utilizing a few key principles.

Principle One
Know the outcomes of a meeting before it starts.

When you do, you'll know when you have finished! When you are finished, adjourn! Here are three examples of possible outcomes.

- *Information must be presented, comprehended, and supported.* Careful consideration in such a meeting should be given to the media used, the recapitulation of key facts, and a means of calculating the commitment established.

- *A decision must be reached.* This kind of meeting must be planned to allow discussion and questions as well as a mechanism for establishing consensus. Careful planning will lead to a successful, clear decision. Difficulties can be created when a decision is not reached.

- *Training must be accomplished.* Training meetings can either be fun and interesting, or boring and distasteful. Planning appropriate methods and materials can make all the difference.

- *A problem must be solved.* A meeting of this nature can be daunting, even scary, but unnecessarily so. If a problem-solving process is employed and the group carefully facilitated, solving problems can be a very satisfying experience.

Principle Two
Prepare the room and the people for success.

- Develop the agenda simply and logically to accomplish the purpose of the meeting.
- Arrange the room to accommodate the purpose of the meeting. If there is a media presentation, all chairs should be facing the front. If there are documents to work through, meeting around tables works. If there is discussion or consensus involved, meeting in a circle or around a large table may be necessary. Prepare the room.

Principle Three
Facilitate!

When leading a meeting, it is critical that the leader moves the meeting toward its intended goal. The leader must know the agenda, when conversations are extraneous, when a side issue should be acknowledged and left for an additional meeting, and when one person is dominating the meeting and how to manage such a person. The leader can't get caught in the weeds but must facilitate the predetermined objective.

Conflict Resolution

One Organization in this world where conflict should be most easily resolved is the Organization where it is most regularly left unresolved. It is often left unresolved because the members of the Organization have never been taught a simple, effective method for resolving it. Those who bear the fruit of the Spirit and speak the Love Language of Companionship should be experts at this, but it is not generally the case.

In churches that lack this skill, wounds can be found that have lasted for years or generations among staff, leaders, and members. That's especially sad when the intent of The Boss is that the ultimate attribute characterizing His church is a humble, forgiving, and forbearing love.

Training in conflict resolution should be availed to every member of the Organization. The process is simple and can be learned by anyone, although there will always be a few who believe it's beyond their understanding or ability. Websites abound with detailed information on this subject, but here are seven basic principles.

Step One: Be the Listener.

In any conflict, the one who listens most, and best is the one who will ultimately lead the resolution. The one who talks or emotes the most is more apt to continue the conflict. Take notes and recapitulate the issues until real understanding is established. Without understanding, progress halts

Step Two: Allow Time for Emotional Release.

When people are in conflict, one or the other or both people are usually seeking a place where they can let off steam. The amount of emotion connected with this emotional release usually does not match the size or scope of the issue involved. This happens when a person is packing some other unresolved issues in their life. In any case, allowing a person the space and time to let their emotions out without argument or recourse helps diffuse the tension that may exist.

Step Three: Discover the Root Cause.

The problem that creates the conflict is often merely a symptom of the real cause that is beneath it. It is important that honesty and openness lead to the discovery of the root cause. More listening, recapitulation, and humility will be required and important during this step.

Step Four: Find Common Ground.

The reason for conflict is usually narrow, even small. There may be many areas where common ground and agreement already exist between two people, so it is important to find these areas of agreement and highlight them. These can be values, purposes, or perspectives and there are probably many to be found when one looks for them!

Step Five: Find a Compromise.

Compromise does not mean giving up either principles or policies. It means that progress forward can benefit both people if a win/win compromise is established between them. Each person will need to give a little to gain a little. There can be no winners and losers in conflict resolution. A person who feels the need to win every time they are in a conflict is known as a bully.

Step Six: Establish Measurements.

Once an agreement is reached, some form of measurement needs to be put into place. The two parties need to agree on the behavior that will demonstrate that the conflict is truly resolved. It is important to establish a timeframe, a future date when the resolution will be measured for its success.

Step Seven: Close the Loop.

At some point closure should be celebrated. It is good to have a time to celebrate a "remember when" moment bringing complete closure to the issue.

Expectations Management

If we all work to please One Boss, why do so many vocational ministers fail, burn out, or quit because of discouragement, disillusionment, even depression? The answer isn't nearly as complicated as it's made to seem. Most of the time the answer lies in taking control of an area of work that is within the grasp of everyone who works in the Management layer of the Organization, the area of expectations!

The same work has the power to delight and disappoint based on the expectations that were established for it. If I promise someone that they will have my work on a project by Wednesday, and then deliver it to them on Thursday, regardless of how well it's done, it will create disappointment. If, however, I deliver the same exact work to my project manager on Tuesday, it will create delight. The SAME work! The difference was the expectations that were created before I even began.

Taking control of expectations is a tool anyone can use and has tremendous power to create happy clients, workers, and co-workers. It all has to do with the expectations that were established and successfully met. We should note that unclear expectations are the source of more discouragement in an Organization that anyone might imagine. The phrase, "I'm not sure what I'm expected to do," is a killer in any organization, particularly the church. Be assured, volunteers won't tolerate it. When working with volunteers, Ministry Leaders must take care to give them the opportunity to do work that delights! This happens when expectations are clear, and those expectations are accompanied by adequate training.

There are three factors that make expectations clear. These are quantity, quality, and time. People who work want to know how much they should do to be successful, how well they should do it, and when it needs to be done. How much? How well? When? When these three factors are clear, everyone is given the opportunity to create work that delights.

In any layer of the Organization, the church needs to get away from thinking that everyone has to be pleased with everything that is done. We all work to please One Boss! When a Ministry Leader gives a group in the Organization an opportunity to speak one or more of the Six Love Languages, all that remains is clear expectations and training to be successful!

The Seven Habits of Highly Effective People

The personal habits of successful people were studied and put into print in 1989 by Stephen Covey in his highly acclaimed book, The Seven Habits of Highly Effective People. Corporations have taught them in one form or another ever since. The source and study of these habits have been discussed and debated ad nauseum but have never been discredited.

The wonder is that the church has never adopted them when not one of these habits runs contrary to the leading of The Boss! They are simply good ways of ordering the inner world of people to make their work effective in any organization. Why not the church?

I am confident they have morphed a little in my application of them over the years, but my confidence in them remains steadfast. They are listed here with my personal twist on each one as skills worth developing in the leadership layers of the church.

1. Be Proactive.

One of my sons is an intelligence officer in the United States Navy. We've tried to summarize his job in many ways, but always come back to, "Get out in front of whatever just happened." That's the way proactive people function. As they see what has happened, may happen, or could happen, they are already forming a plan to meet the next challenge before it happens.

They are solution-oriented people who don't peddle problems through the Organization. Instead, they prepare solutions for every eventuality. They are fun to work with because they are positive people, always looking for a way forward.

2. Begin with the End in Mind.

This attribute applies not only to how effective people do their work, but how they grow personally. These people see who they want to become and put steps in place as they grow into just that person. They envision a future and pursue it. This habit affects everything they do, down to the simplest tasks. It makes them fun to work with because they are confident and full of answers to questions. They know where they are going and how they are going to get there.

3. Put First Things First.

Have you ever spent time around people who seem to have it all together? They eat the right things, exercise in all the right ways, think the right thoughts, and do the right things. As long as they stay humble, they are like Rabbis from whom to learn how to order life. They become this kind of person by putting priorities in place and sticking with them. Every day they do the things that will contribute to long-term success. You never find them caught in the tyranny of the urgent. They seem to be able to handle emergencies and distractions with a calm assurance. They have learned to keep the main thing the main thing.

4. Think Win/Win.

These people offer positive outcomes to others as they pursue their own. In planning, problem-solving, or compromise they continuously find paths forward that give those around them wins as they successfully accomplish their own goals. You will not find these people creating silos in the Organization in which they can isolate themselves. They do not demand that methods or policies work only for themselves.

They are creative people who work well with others because they find ways forward that benefit everyone. They make excellent leaders because they find successful paths on which everyone can walk.

5. Seek First to Understand; then to Be Understood.

Nothing builds social connections faster or better than understanding. King Solomon taught that the value found in understanding others can't be measured. People with this habit take time to listen! They are able to withstand the outbursts that sometimes happen while work is accomplished. You often hear people with this habit saying the phrase, "Let me see if I understand what you are telling me." They seldom use the word, "but" in the middle of a conversation.

This habit causes a person to wait to open themselves up to the thoughts of others before speaking in response. This habit does not mean sacrificing the ideals or principles on which the Organization has agreed; but it does mean finding out where people are before attempting to show them where they need to be.

6. Synergize.

People with this habit pull others in around them as they pursue their goals. They find roles for others to participate with them on their projects. They are good delegators. It's fun to work on their teams because they make expectations clear and find ways to allow others to be creative in accomplishing them. They are salespersons of ideas and values. They convince you of their goals and your value to them as a team member who will join with them to progress toward them. No one dreads working with or for people with this habit.

7. Sharpen the Saw.

People with this habit know what they know, as well as what they don't and in response, are constantly working to learn the things that will help them succeed. They also want to learn new skills as they go forward.

They are not intimidated by new systems or methods because learning new things is always seen as interesting challenges to them. If they find deficiencies in their own abilities, they acknowledge them and find ways to remedy them. Working around them is a pleasure because they will expose those who work with them to all kinds of possibilities and opportunities to grow simply because that's the way they live!

Problem-Solving Methods

Churches seem unaware that problem-solving methods have existed in corporations for years. During the Quality Revolution in the 1980s, groups of problem-solvers were called quality circles or continuous improvement teams. They were cross sectional groups of employees gathered to solve issues of accuracy, speed, or coordination in business processes.

Rare is the church that has either discovered or utilizes existing problem-solving processes. What is typically found in the church are issues, which are discussed and tabled at monthly standing meetings rarely leading to resolution. Most of the time the meetings occur infrequently enough that inordinate amounts of time are wasted in repetitive explanations. At any given meeting, little progress is made and that progress is quickly forgotten.

In many corporations, skilled groups of problem solvers may become so efficient at working an internal problem solving process that the same groups of people are asked to solve varieties of problems. Problem-solving teams go through four stages as they become experts. These are forming, storming, norming, and performing.

- **Forming**
  As problem-solving teams form, there is a spirit of enthusiasm, excitement, and anticipation in the team.

- **Storming**

  The team discovers varieties of giftedness and approach to the problem- solving process and the storms begin to brew.

- **Norming**

  The group finds its rhythm and the skill sets that will make them successful.

- **Performing**

  When a team has performed the problem-solving process once, they become skilled performers at handling any issue given to them.

It all comes down to the utilization of an effective process. What follows are the principles involved in the major steps of an effective problem-solving process. Varieties of these kinds of processes can be downloaded from the Internet where they abound.

Step One: Identify the Issue

For example, a business may be making widgets with 95% accuracy, which means that 5% of what they make is scrap. Therefore, an issue, which becomes the mission for a problem-solving team might be to reduce scrap by 50%, which would result in an accuracy of 97.5%. An example in the church might be that it takes too long to register our children on Sunday mornings. A mission statement for a church team might be to reduce the time it takes to register our children by 50%.

Step Two: Brainstorm the Root Causes

This session would involve the team generating as many ideas as possible regarding the issue they've been given. In our church example, all the causes for the slowdown of registering children would have to be generated.

Step Three: Build Consensus

An analysis of the root causes will tend to congregate around four issues: Man, Machine, Method, or Material.

- **Man**: In our church example, untrained volunteers are slowing down the process or volunteers are engaging in lengthy conversations at the registration desk.
- **Machine: Outdated** technology or lack of technology slows down the process and causing personnel to use cumbersome paper forms.
- **Method: People** are lining up in a long, narrow hallway, which causes everyone to register their children one at a time.
- **Material: Lack** of signage is creating confusion leading to age- grouping problems so that after long waits, kids and their parents may end up in the wrong line.

Regardless of where they group, causes will tend to congregate around one of these four issues. The problem-solving team uses a technique called multi-voting to determine which of these issues is creating most of the problems. There may be more than one contributor.

Step Four: Write a Problem Statement

Sufficient wordsmithing is given to this step to very accurately describe the target of the problem to be solved. The identified root causes must be at the heart of this statement. In our church example, a problem statement might read, "Inefficiencies at the registration desk are creating a bottleneck in the child registration process."

Step Five: Brainstorm Solutions

The group generates ideas as solutions to the problem statement. It is possible at this step that data may need to be gathered. In our church example, the average time it takes to register a child may need to be measured. At the close of this step, consensus is built around the best solution or solutions (more multi-voting).

Step Six: Analyze the Solution

The solutions generated may create ancillary problems, costs, or other prohibitive factors. Obviously, the solution must have a net benefit.

Step Seven: Create an Implementation Plan

- The team builds a model of how the implemented solution functions.
- The team generates a list of all the points of communication and training it will take to implement the plan.

Step Eight: Create Success Measurements

The group decides how success will be measured and a duration to determine the implementation is fully established.

Step Nine: Execute the Plan

The group determines a launch date, training dates, technology upgrades, process improvements, etc. that can be launched at a particular time and launches them.

Step Ten: Measure the Results

The group measures the differences between what was happening before and after executing their solutions. They look for intended consequences, which were targeted by their solutions, and unintended consequences, which may yield results they weren't anticipating. The intended consequence may fail, but hopefully not. Regardless, the improvement needs to be measured. In our church example, one unintended consequence might be reduced interaction between parents of young children.

Step Eleven: Follow-Up

- When finishing its work, the problem-solving team needs to both celebrate and debrief. If the team is ever asked to work on another problem, what would they do differently? How could they be more efficient? How could they be more effective? During this debriefing session, the team can determine whether or not they would be willing to solve future problems.
- The team needs to keep measuring their implemented solution. The only way to assure compliance with the new process is to keep measuring it. Old habits tend to die hard.

Brainstorming

People still talk about brainstorming, and some even say that they implement it from time to time, but it is rarely used as it was originally intended to be used. At its heart brainstorming is a free and open environment where ideas are generated without editorials or limits. When properly executed the participants feel free to toss into the pool of ideas anything that might come to mind. Some sessions are suspended, then resume to allow participants to gather ideas from various sources.

Those sources might include other churches or groups who are working with a similar process, someone might attend a seminar where certain skills are being taught, or sometimes ideas can come from dissimilar functions which have developed patterns that can be interpolated into the church. Regardless, real brainstorming is not limited by time or traditions. Brainstorms are used to think outside the box. As any good song writer would tell you, never throw away a good line, rhyme, or hook because at some point it may come back to be very valuable.

Facilitators of brainstorming sessions need to be skilled in group dynamics in several ways.
- They must familiarize themselves with the issue around which the storm will gather sufficient to keep energy in the room when it begins to wane. Brainstorming gets its name and effectiveness through symbiotic energy as one idea leads to another within the group.

- They must understand that there are truly no bad ideas while the storm is ongoing. Every idea generated must be treated and noted as having value. The person generating the idea must be encouraged to keep thinking creatively and expansively.
- Editorial comments must be kept out of the room. Limits of time, budget, and human capital are never factored while brainstorming is ongoing. Phrases like, "That will never work because…" must be silenced.
- They must keep a careful ear out for protectionism. There may be people in the group whose processes may be more greatly affected by certain ideas than by others, and these people may try to direct the discussion toward ideas that are either less burdensome or more supportive of their own work.
- They must be ready to inject new thoughts into the group if the ideas begin to all fall into one category or they simply grind to a halt. Re-energizing the group is critical until there is a complete brain drain among the members of the group. This means the facilitator must keep moving the group toward new thoughts until it is obvious no new thoughts exist in their ranks.

Every idea must be captured and returned to the group after the session closes. Sometimes the best ideas come after a session has ended and the members of the team are reviewing their work. Brainstorming teams must not be afraid to keep the storm brewing until they have exhausted themselves. Only then can evaluation of the ideas begin.

A light, celebratory feeling should be cultivated in the room where brainstorming occurs. It may help to have huge rolls of writing paper on tables to allow group members to move freely about the room and jot down their ideas as they announce them to the team. Feeding teams while they brainstorm is always a good idea. Preparing the room with pictures or graphics that keep the issue around which the storm should gather always before the team is a good idea. To be creative, participants must feel they are in a creative environment.

Building Consensus

In the church, voting is one of the least effective ways to either make decisions or build consensus. In our government, we have decided that a majority rules philosophy of progress should exist. This philosophy has been adopted by many Organizations that would be much better off building consensus by other means. As can be seen by many congressional and supreme court decisions, voting creates more division about issues than it creates any amount of consensus. This is the reason minority opinions were developed. A minority opinion is simply a rationale for the statement, "I didn't vote for that," which is a statement that should never be uttered in the church.

In the church, falling back on the statement, "I didn't vote for that," is spoken to the detriment of several critical factors.
- It means that the vote on whatever issue was decided by it is the pivotal point of control in the Organization. This

means that control of the Organization has effectively been taken out of the hands of The Boss. It would be difficult to number the times in the biblical record when a vote would have sent God's children in a direction diametrically opposed to His will. The Boss of the church must always be held in the position of control in His Organization.

- Voting leaves open the possibility of creating enduring factions in the church. Unity is one of the marks of the working of the Holy Spirit in the church. Jesus prayed for just such unity and Paul taught specifically against factions in the church. Unity is a mark of maturity and division a mark of immaturity. Using a decision-making method that not only permits division to exist, but in some cases empowers it means that surely another method of consensus-building must be availed.

- Voting undermines the effectiveness of the Organizational structure of the church. The kinds of questions voting precipitates chisel at the cooperative functionality that must exist in the church. Who gets to vote? Why don't I get to vote on certain issues? Why do certain people vote on some issues, but not others? How do I get myself into a role that allows me to vote?

  Who or when were the policies voted into place and what does it take to change them? Every one of these questions tear at the fabric of what makes the church the church yet voting constantly brings them to mind. I am confident I have not exhausted the reasons why voting does not build consensus in the church but is detrimental to it.

People who see the functionality of the church from different points of view cannot be purged from the Organization, nor should they be. What must exist between all leaders who seek the direction of The Boss is the willingness to concede to, abide by, and bond with perspectives not their own. A process must be used that allows maximum opportunity for expression of opinion as well as the greatest opportunity for agreeable conclusions. Two are superior to voting.

Unanimity of Support

Getting people to agree to support a decision or perspective is much easier than getting their approval. Stop asking for approval and start asking for support. Support requires only a level of agreement greater than the conviction of the opposition offered by the other individuals responsible for the decision. When determining the direction of The Boss, everyone at the table need not be an advocate of it. They merely need to see its validity to the point of giving it their support. Only when an individual cannot give even nominal support to an idea do they need to object to it.

Otherwise, unanimous support should be achievable for any idea. When unanimity cannot be reached, further time needs to be spent with The Boss seeking His direction. Every decision must be made in the temperament and conduct required by The Boss and must demonstrate its connection to speaking one or more of the Six Love Languages to Him.

This is the specific conviction of support every decision-maker must come under to render effective decisions for the Organization. If unanimous consent cannot be reached by this method, there is another; however, the effort to reach unanimous support should be given time, prayer, fasting, and exhaustive soul- searching with The Boss before a secondary method is employed.

Expression of Support

There are times when opposition to one idea may be so strong, or support for multiple ideas so divided that a different kind of consensus building method needs to be used.

There are times when two kinds of log jams cannot be overcome.

- One log jam is when discussion after discussion leads to no clear consensus. Churches notoriously table issues that cannot be resolved with discussions. Opportunistic leaders use these situations to exert their control when no clear path forward seems obvious. Sometimes these grabs for control are couched in theological terms so that anyone in the room with less scriptural knowledge than the controller is left shrinking into the corners of the discussion.

   At other times, a person with substantial personal influence exerts his or her control of the group. If the group is strong enough to forestall these kinds of individuals, they have no way forward except to continue to table issues for months on end and nothing is resolved.
- Another log jam results when one or more members of the group have personal interest or investment in the outcome and simply ignore the discussions in an effort to prolong a decision that wears down the group. Out of frustration, the group is forced to agree with members

that are not seeking the leading and control of The Boss but are simply imposing their will on the group.

In these cases, a method exists to break the log jam. After significant soul- searching, prayer, and seeking the leading of the Holy Spirit, a group is either deciding between two possibilities or cannot bring focus on the best or worst possibility among several, the group is offered a number of points to assign to every possibility that has merit. These may be problems, root causes, possible solutions, or varying visions.

Every person is given the same number of points that represent the depth of their conviction about each of the possibilities. For example: if 50 points are given to

each person, person 1 may think each of three possibilities has nearly equal merit, so he divides his points 15 for one, 15 for another, and 20 for the third. Person 2 thinks one possibility has significantly more merit than the other two, so she assigns her points, 25 for one and 12.5 for each of the others.

Two rules must be followed. No person may assign more than half their points to any given possibility, but each person is free to assign less than their full allotment of 50 points to all the possibilities. This keeps any individual from piling all the allotted points on one possibility in an attempt to exert greater influence on the outcome of their choice. Therefore, person 3 may put 25 points on one possibility and 1 on another and zero on the third.

The facilitator totals up the points and gives the totals to the group. These can be written anonymously, if necessary. A consensus of thought will appear in the statistics. Either one possibility will separate itself from the other two, or two will rise above the one. It is possible that all three will remain close to each other. When this occurs, each should be studied individually again for their merit before repeating the exercise.

Several good things come from this exercise. In silence, consensus of thought is realized! The actual differences in the group's opinions are visible in numeric proportions. Every person in the room exerts equal influence on the outcome, so there can be no arguing with the conclusion.

It is possible this kind of exercise may need to be repeated two or three times to reach consensus of support and at its conclusion, unanimous consent must be established with its outcome.

If a given individual persistently finds himself or herself with a differing opinion to the group, it may be necessary to privately discuss the vision of the leadership team with this individual and their value to the group questioned. Prayer, fasting, and gentleness need to go into such a conversation.

When a decision is reached by a leadership group, that group must speak to the Organization about it with one voice. It is imperative that by whatever means, unanimity is reached, and every member of the group recognizes their own personal support for the conclusion as the leading of The Boss!

Continuous Improvement (TQM) through Benchmarking

In great companies, failure or weakness is always viewed as an opportunity to improve. If employees are afraid to fail, they will not take risks nor will they be honest about their need to improve. The need to please a supervisor, or at least not disappoint one, is the inner influence that keeps most employees from exposing their weaknesses and failures. In every successful organization where creativity and innovation are important, it is critical to establish an environment of continuous improvement. People need to feel that their failures will not be punished but used as points of reference for improvement. This is a cultural atmosphere that must be cultivated.

This should not be foreign to the church. Our Boss treats our failures with grace and forgiveness when we are faithful to confess our sins to Him. It is only when we try to hide from Him that we get ourselves into a destructive frame of mind. It is the same with the culture of the church. Everyone who works in The Boss's Organization must feel the freedom to try, risk, and venture out even if they fail, knowing that failure will be met with grace and the opportunity to improve.

The key to continuous improvement is the depth of honesty with which we agree to look at our failures. The skill of benchmarking enters the work process at this specific point of honesty. All too often we jump forward with change in the Organization without first examining what is going on in the processes that are driving it forward. The fix is implemented before the process is analyzed. Benchmarking means taking measurements that reveal what is happening currently before plunging into change simply for the sake of making things different.

This example is an actual case study. A receptionist was assigned clerical work in addition to her work at the front desk where she also answers all incoming phone calls. She was struggling to accomplish the assigned clerical work, so a time study was made to discover all that was keeping her from completing her tasks. It is important to understand that the time study was NOT an effort to improve her situation but was only implemented to accurately understand the inputs to her day that might be keeping her from her goal. Her failure was never seen as something personal, but only something to be studied to see how her environment could be improved. It was viewed as an opportunity!

For one week, she wrote down every input to her day, and how long each lasted. How many guests did she greet and direct into the office? How many phone calls did she receive? How many characters did she type? How many interruptions occurred? How long did each interruption last? In which parts of the day did each of these inputs occur?

Her capable administrative skills, welcoming personality, and pleasant appearance were factors that had made her perfect for her role as receptionist when she was hired. Her personality and appearance made her a frequent stop for many of the male employees who would gather at her desk to chat! Other factors came to light as well and an accurate picture was developed regarding the pace and particulars of her work. A benchmark was established. We were able to conclude exactly what was happening to her as she attempted to accomplish all that was assigned to her. Percentages were given to each of the factors we measured (handling phone calls, greeting and directing guests, clerical tasks, interruptions, etc.)

The resulting changes were impressive. She was able to restructure her days to accomplish all that she had been assigned and more. This resulted from first establishing a benchmark. When she understood that she needed not be afraid of exposing everything that was causing her to fail, she was willing to allow the benchmark to be established and significant improvement resulted. She was much happier being able to succeed and the office got more work from her than expected.

An unintended consequence was that more of the male employees who were trained not to loiter at the front desk accomplished more of their own work, too! Benchmarking is not simply time studies. Any process in the church can be studied for its effectiveness based on a variety of factors. The key is building a culture in which everyone involved does not fear the benchmarking process. The culture must see their environment as a place where continuous improvement is a way of life!

Note: The three phases of discipline that any church worker may undergo were explained previously. Those phases are employed only after repeated failure discovered through multiple conversations and a benchmarking process has been implemented.

Performance Evaluations

Paul said to the Thessalonians that his ministry to and among them was done not to please the Thessalonians or anyone else. It was done to please The Boss! The Bible admonishes every Christian to work as unto the Lord no matter what the work is.

The Bible even explains how masters and slaves relate to one another when working to demonstrate their Christianity while working together. In the church, all work is done at the direction of The Boss and for His pleasure. When every person in the church works in this fashion, there should be no fear meeting with a spiritually mature person to talk about it.

It is important to understand why performance evaluations are both necessary and helpful to the Organization. Here are a few critical factors for handling them in the church where everyone is working for The Boss!

- No surprises!

    Evaluations should be conducted once every year concurrent with the development of the Master Plan for the next year. Each person undergoing an evaluation is allowed to look at themselves and their current efforts as they think about what they will do in the coming year.

- No surprises!

    If performance problems have been observed in any given worker in the church, those problems should have been addressed at the time and not saved up for a formal, annual evaluation. Timely performance feedback is critical for the encouragement, as well as the correction of anyone working in the church.

- No surprises!

  Everyone works for The Boss in the church. Therefore, every worker is allowed to evaluate themselves out their own conscience, as guided by the leading of the Holy Spirit.

  Presenting a personal evaluation to a Ministry Leader, Staff Leader, or Executive Team member should feel like an opportunity to expose their heart for their Boss, not as an occasion for criticism from a staff member of the church.

What follows is an explanation of what each question of the evaluation is attempting to expose to every worker in the church. Every worker should be given the privilege to do this! Here is a review of the questions.

- While submitting to the leading of the Holy Spirit, how well have my efforts helped the church speak the Six Love Languages to The Boss?

  This question allows a worker to see the connection between their work and the accomplishment of the mission of the Organization. Even the smallest tasks accomplished by a worker in the church should reflect their connection to one or more of the Six Love Languages spoken to The Boss. This question opens an opportunity to reinvigorate and encourage the worker because of their contribution to the overall purpose of the Organization.

- Having established my own success criteria in my areas of responsibility, how well did I hit my targets for the year?

  This question allows the worker to self-deprecate. Have they set goals? Have they made good effort? What do they think of themselves and their work? This question also opens the conversation to issues of overload and burnout. Is this worker trying to do too much to the detriment of their own life requirements?

- How is my intimacy with God going? Is my personal walk with Him, connection to Him, and ability to sense His leadership in my life going well?

  If everyone in the Organization knows they work for The Boss, and not for whomever is in the room with them at the time of their evaluation, they should be willing to open up about their intimacy with The Boss. No one should be expected to lead a portion of the Organization to a place where they are absent. Answering this question should open a perfect opportunity for a discussion of John's Accountability Model for intimacy with The Boss.

  Does this person need an accountability partner to help them grow closer to The Boss?

- How clearly do I see the vision and goals for my areas of responsibility? Is the leadership of The Boss and my understanding of the expectations I am trying to meet giving me a clear picture of what I am attempting to accomplish?

  As has been previously noted, one of the most detrimental work environments is one in which the expectations are unclear. If clear vision has not been cast by the description of responsibilities they've been given, now is the time to clarify it. No one in the church should suffer from the indignity of not understanding what is expected of them. This question also works well with plans for the upcoming year. If changes are going to be projected, this is a good place for their ideals to be discussed.

- Am I still fully engaged with the people with whom I serve? Do we laugh, cry, discuss, and make decisions together freely and openly?

  The church is a people-helping Organization. If a worker is discouraged or struggling with relationships, this question should help unearth their struggle. None of the gifts of ministry described in Romans 12 can be utilized without functioning with or alongside others. A worker that disengages from people may be crying out for help.

- How would I rate my personal passion for ministry in general at this juncture?

  Ministry is a unique function because the struggles occur now, and the rewards occur later. It takes great passion for The Boss, His interests, and His objectives in order to continuously motivate workers in His Organization. If passion for ministry begins to fade, only the struggles will remain. The joy in serving The Boss comes from an individual's love for Him and desire to see His kingdom succeed.

- Are there new areas of ministry toward which The Boss is leading me as I view my long-range future with this Organization? If so, what are they?

    As people grow in Christ, their interests may change. It is important to see that the leading of The Boss in the life of an individual is His possible leading of the ministry direction of the local church. There is only one Holy Spirit, and He is not divided against Himself, nor will He ever be. When a Ministry Leader expresses interest in a new area of responsibility, it is possible that the Holy Spirit is leading the church in that direction. For the sake of long- range planning and the sustaining of the continuity of ministry efforts, it is important to open this conversation with Ministry Leaders at least once every year.

Human Resources Training

People who work in the church should not be ignorant of the functions of Human Resources (HR). HR departments exist in all businesses to act as an advocate for the employees, as well as to perform particular services for their companies. These departments typically manage services such as: compensation packages, benefits packages, hiring and firing processes, personnel files, employee discipline plans, negotiating insurance and other benefits, arbitrating employee grievances, and offering training in areas of employee skills, as well as safety and harassment.

HR staff offer new employees orientation training. They work with their IT departments to explain computer functionality, such as file structures and nomenclature. They also set internet usage policies and applicable punishments for abuses. HR staff members understand labor laws and how they apply to equitability for all employees regardless of their minority status.

They understand liability issues and how to protect their employees, as well as their businesses. They do regular background checks on their employees, keeping them current. They oversee ADA compliance, as well as fire safety of buildings for their employees and through it all, they are expected to continuously lengthen employee retention, improve employee morale, and be ready with a pipeline full of replacements as turnover occurs. They really are amazing people!

Anyone working in any of the leadership layers of the church should be made aware of how the human resource functions work in their Organization. If necessary, worker handbooks can be written, distributed, and kept up to date.

It is rare in the church to receive training in HR functions, but it is important. At the very least, training in office safety and sexual harassment should be conducted annually and made mandatory for employees of the church.

The internet has many sources for copious amounts of information about HR functions. Suffice it here to note its importance to the church and its workers.

CHAPTER 15
Where Do I Begin?

If you have endured my book to this point, I hope two things are true for you. First, that you aren't bored to death, and that at least some of what you have read, you have found relevant to your church. Second, I hope you are at least a little inspired to try a few of the new things you've learned. If I were you, and I was thinking of implementing many of these concepts that may be different from the management environment in the church you serve, I'd be asking myself where to begin. This chapter of the book is written to give you some ideas about the starting point and significant mileposts that may help you.

If you have been noting the principles, processes, and plans outlined thus far, you have recognized that implementing them cannot be an all at once effort. The significant teaching and re-orienting of traditional thinking, though necessary, will not occur with a weekend retreat or sermon series. What follows is a guide, not a hard and fast process. Each church will have strengths and weaknesses that will require more attention to some actions and less to others.

Begin by entering into partnerships between Staff Leaders and members of the Executive Team by using John's Accountability Model for Increasing Intimacy with God and Preparing for the Language of Evangelism. It is intimacy with God, The Boss, that is the single most important part of creating success in church management, no matter what.

Obtain a copy of Jack Taylor's book, *The Hallelujah Factor*. Study the concept of praise in worship and plan to preach a series of sermons on this subject. During the series, plan and coordinate some new patterns or experiences during the worship service. These may include placing different elements in different orders or giving them more attention, incorporating new expressions of worship as they are taught in the sermons, or using unique instrumentation that matches what is being taught in the sermon, such as an acapella Sunday when teaching about Paul and Silas singing on their jail cell. The point is to increase authenticity, expression and, passion in the worship service.

Begin teaching the Executive Team the Six Love Languages as the standard of health in the church. Teach them that these will be used as the measures of the church in accomplishing its mission. Preach a sermon series on each of the languages with two to four sermons on each one. This will begin to focus the church on its priorities.

Get a copy of Ken Hemphill's book, *The Names of God*. Prepare and preach a sermon series on as many of God's Names as possible, which may take approximately 15 weeks. This will prepare everyone for positioning or repositioning God as The Boss of the Organization.

Using the seven questions, prepare and make a first attempt at a Master Plan for the church. Do not be discouraged or disappointed if you do not achieve 100% participation. If necessary, include blank pages (place holders) in the completed plan, but do not fail to include submissions from every Ministry Leader in the process. Publish the plan and allow the whole Organization access to it when it's complete. This will allow the church to see the intentionality of ministry efforts being attempted and produced by the church. It will also give the Executive Team its first opportunity to measure the health of the Organization by comparing the Master Plan to the Six Love Languages and respond by talking to The Boss about what they find.

Teach the unwritten code of conduct to the staff and elders and begin to insist on adherence to it in the leadership circles of the church. Get commitment from everyone to allow accountability in these groups as they learn and then follow through on their commitment to it. It will not take long for the Organization to see a difference in the temperament and conduct of their leaders. At the same time, teach all leaders that The Boss is present at every meeting (wherever 2 or more gather in His Name) and His expectation is that conduct during any meeting will exhibit the Fruits of The Spirit in Galatians 5:22-23. Gain commitment from the staff and Executive Team to support this aspect of leadership.

Prior to the next budgeting cycle of the church, conduct a round of Personnel Reviews with the staff of the church. Use the seven questions offered in this book to allow each staff member to evaluate themselves with their Staff Leader and a third person from the Executive Team present.

Let them realize that their Boss truly is God, and that they will be pressed for excellence by Him. Let them feel the support they should from their Staff Leaders and Executive Team.

Pause. The Bible calls this Selah. All these steps should take at least a year to implement. At this point, it would be good to pause and allow the church time to realize all that is changing. Many things presented in this book must be put into place by seeking the leading of The Boss. There is no specific timetable for them, only a sensitivity to the needs of the Organization and the desires of The Boss.

If there are particular problems that should be addressed that are not management issues, use the visioning process to address them. Allow key Ministry Leaders, Staff Leaders, and the Executive Team to meet regularly for a time, to bond and seek God's direction together. Go slowly, step by step, and see where God leads. Keep the whole Organization praying while this process is going on.

This is the sequence I advise you to use to get the basic parts of this management system into place. The leadership must keep their eyes on the desires of The Boss. When leaders take their eyes off Him and focus on each other, the system will begin to break down.

In conclusion, I offer one example of success that has been transformative in the staff culture I serve. Each of our staff meetings has three standing agenda items.

- Each staff member at the table offers a praise for The Boss. During this time each staff member looks into their ministries to find transformations, movements, or life changes that can be attributed to no one other than God. They verbalize praise for the One responsible for the kingdom outcomes in their work.

- Each staff member seated at the table is asked for prayers for the leading of the Holy Spirit in their work. Each one talks about the upcoming week, month, or quarter where plans are being established and expectations created. Notes are taken and prayers continue for the next week by each staff member for all of the other staff members.

- We bear each other's burdens by sharing personal requests for prayers for our families or friends needing encouragement, healing, or restoration. We allow ourselves to be the church to each other and to speak the languages of companionship and compassion to each other. It is a spiritual experience. Many weeks, tears are shed, or laughter and victory break out. Most weeks I leave staff meetings feeling as though I have just experienced the spiritual highlight of my week. On occasion, it's only me who senses it, but other times, it's everyone. Any management system in the church works in proportion to the leaders' ability to allow God to keep His role as the operational leader and controller of it. If nothing else, never forget that.

EPILOGUE

One final thought needs emphasis. The speed, consistency, and depth of the implementation of everything contained in this book is dependent on one critical factor. Beginning with the Executive Team and working its way up through the entire organization there must exist a spirit of humility. Everyone must adopt the following attitude.

I love the success of the whole organization more than I love my role in it. This spirit of humility is described as "the mind of Christ" in Philippians 2:1-8. Two dynamics will result from its presence throughout the organization.

First, the phrase, "that's not my job" will be eliminated. It will be replaced with a spirit of mutual assistance. Everyone will ask how they can be of help to one another. No one will avoid even the simplest tasks, whether they fall inside their sphere of responsibility or not. Whether setting up chairs for an event or filling in preaching In someone's absence, no task will go unaided by others who can help. The character of the church demands that no one stands by while another part of the organization needs their help.

Second, pride is forced out of the Organization. The current business management culture is filled with driven, proud, self-serving, ladder climbing, assertive people who push their egos onto the people they oversee. Such people have no place in the leadership structure of the church. Pride has led to the fall of many successful church leaders, morally, ethically, even legally. When the success of the whole becomes more important to leadership than their position in the Organization, success will follow inevitably.

God's most useful, successful people throughout scripture are characterized by their humility. Never forget that.

GodIsTheBoss.com

www.ingramcontent.com/pod-product-compliance
Lightning Source LLC
Chambersburg PA
CBHW070913120626
46546CB00001B/251